# Amber's Sketchbook: Cave Paintings

A Detailed Coloring Book

By artist A. G Johnson

ISBN-13: 978-1717099433

ISBN-10: 1717099432

Where it's located: Altamira, Spain

When it was made: Between 35,000 and 15,000 BCE

Why I chose it: I love how much detail is incorporated in this bison pictorial. When I saw it I couldn't wait to put my personal style into the mix.

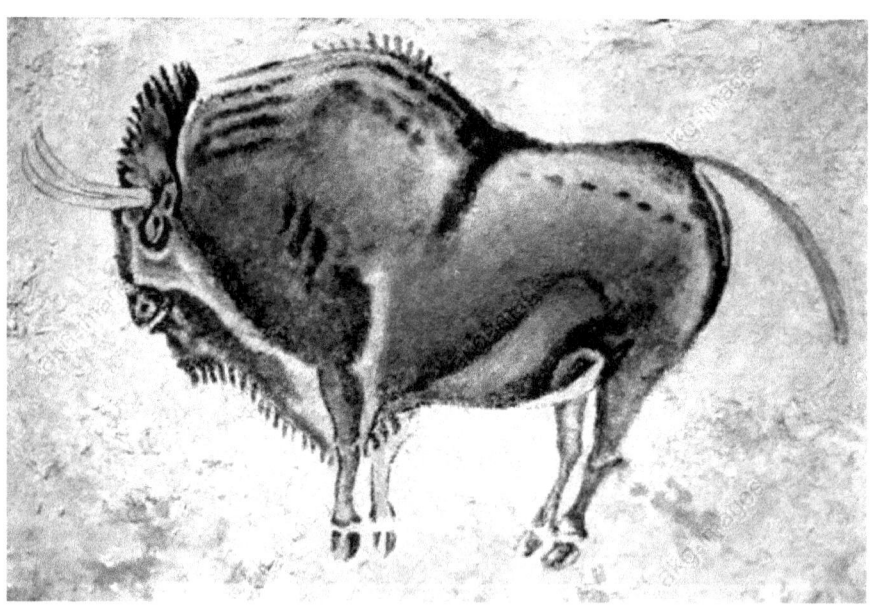

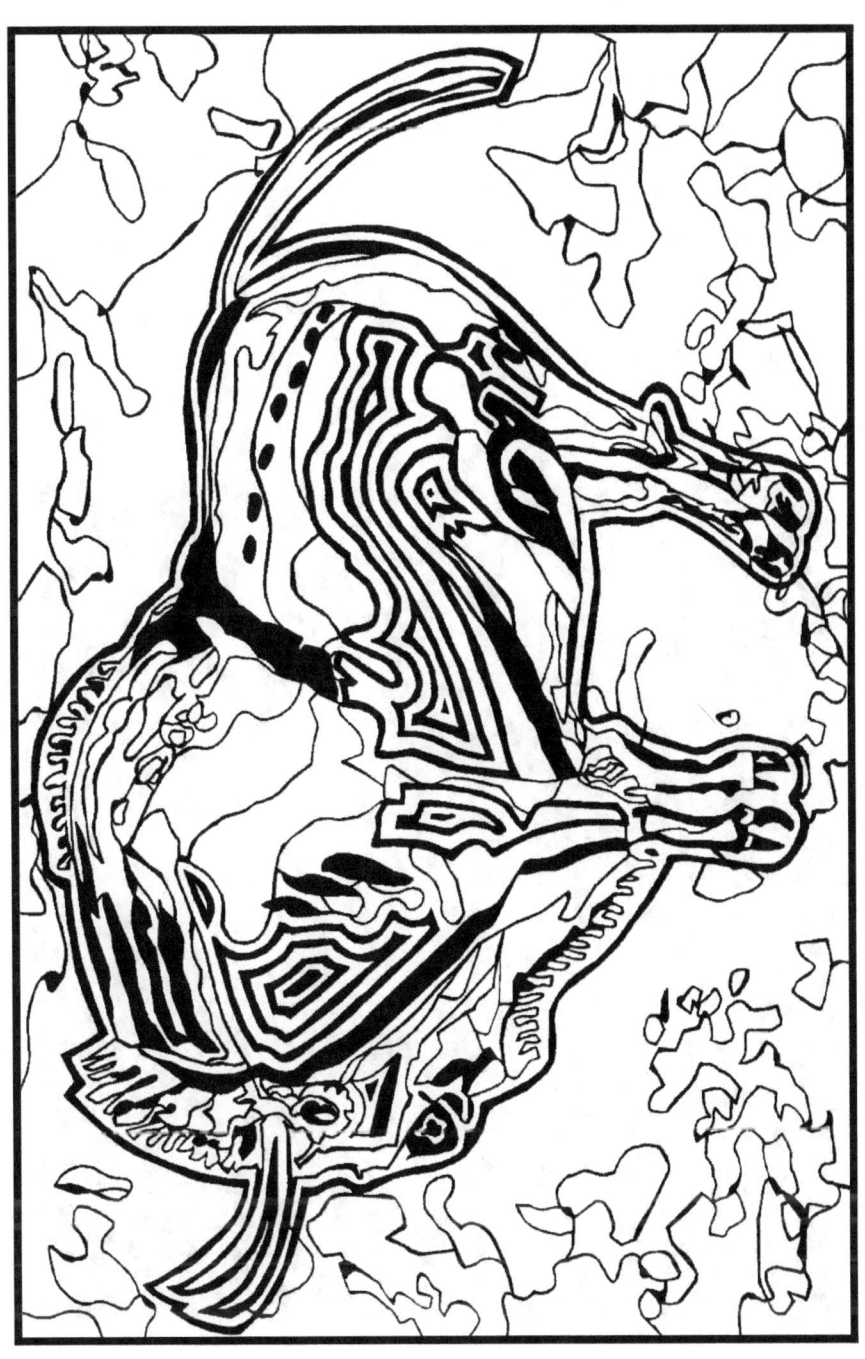

Where it's located: Lascaux, France

When it was made: About 20,000 BCE

Why I chose it: The Lascaux cave paintings are some of the most famous cave paintings around. I loved the way four different animals were captured in this photograph. It makes me want to explore and see what is just beyond the edge of the picture.

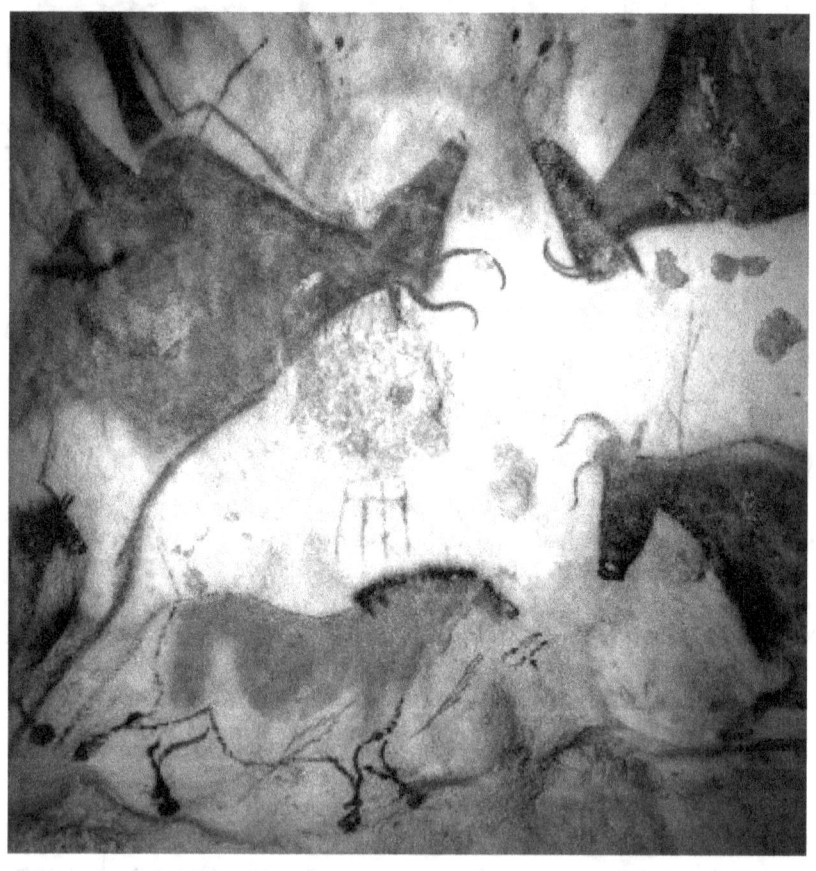

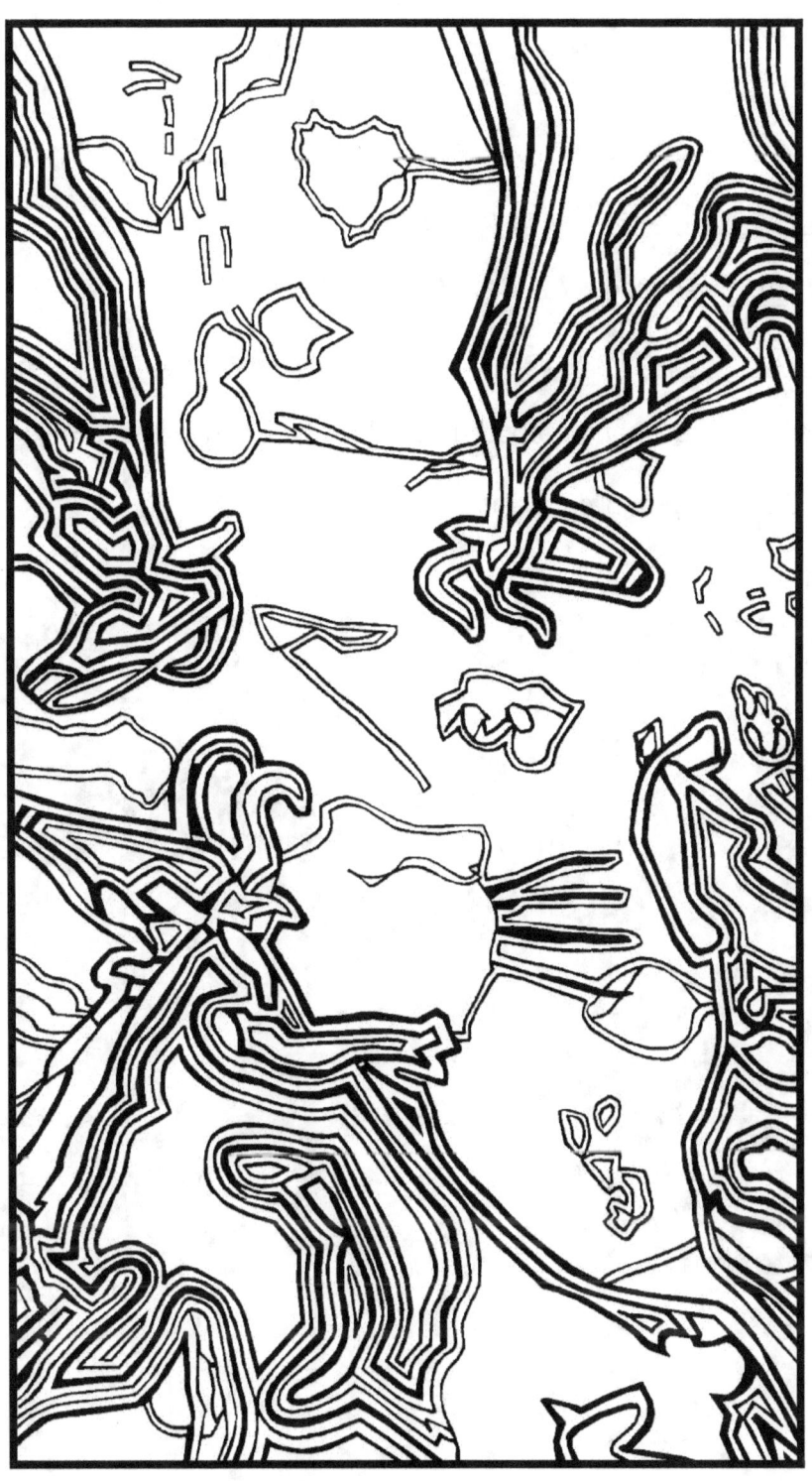

<u>Where it's located</u>: Lascaux, France

<u>When it was made</u>: About 20,000 BCE

<u>Why I chose it</u>: Possible *the* most famous cave painting. It was the first one I learned about in grade school and it has always had a soft spot in my heart

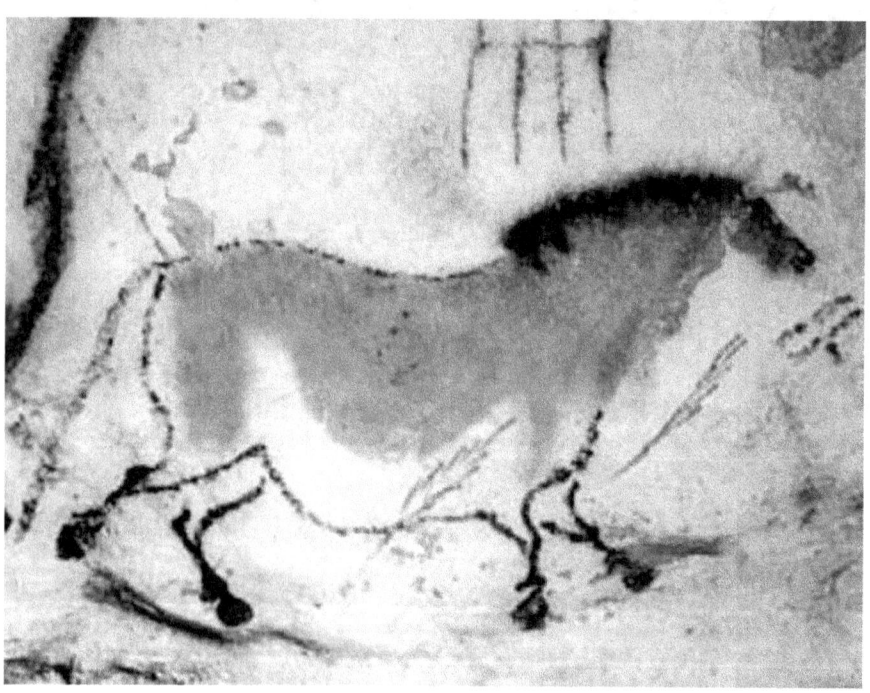

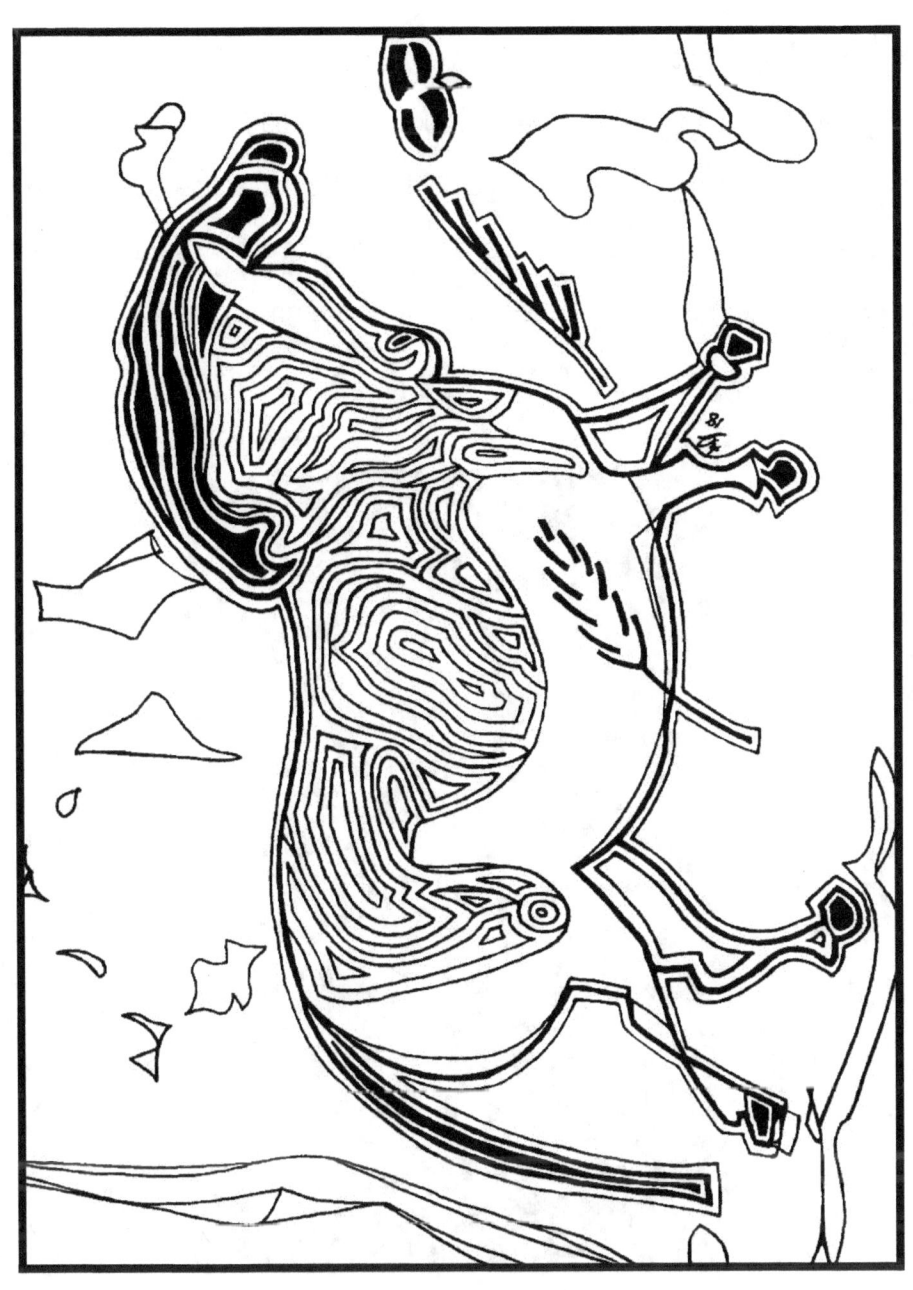

<u>Where it's located:</u> Chauvet-Pont-d'Arc, France

<u>When it was made:</u> Between 36,000 and 30,000 BCE

<u>Why I chose it:</u> I had never seen this particular figure before I started doing research for this collection. I loved how simple the lines are and how effortless it seems, although it probably took hours for the person to create.

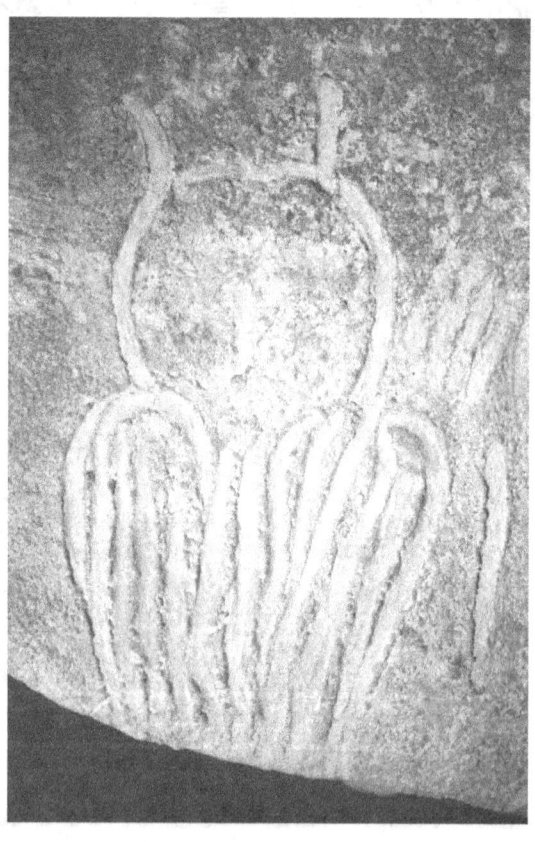

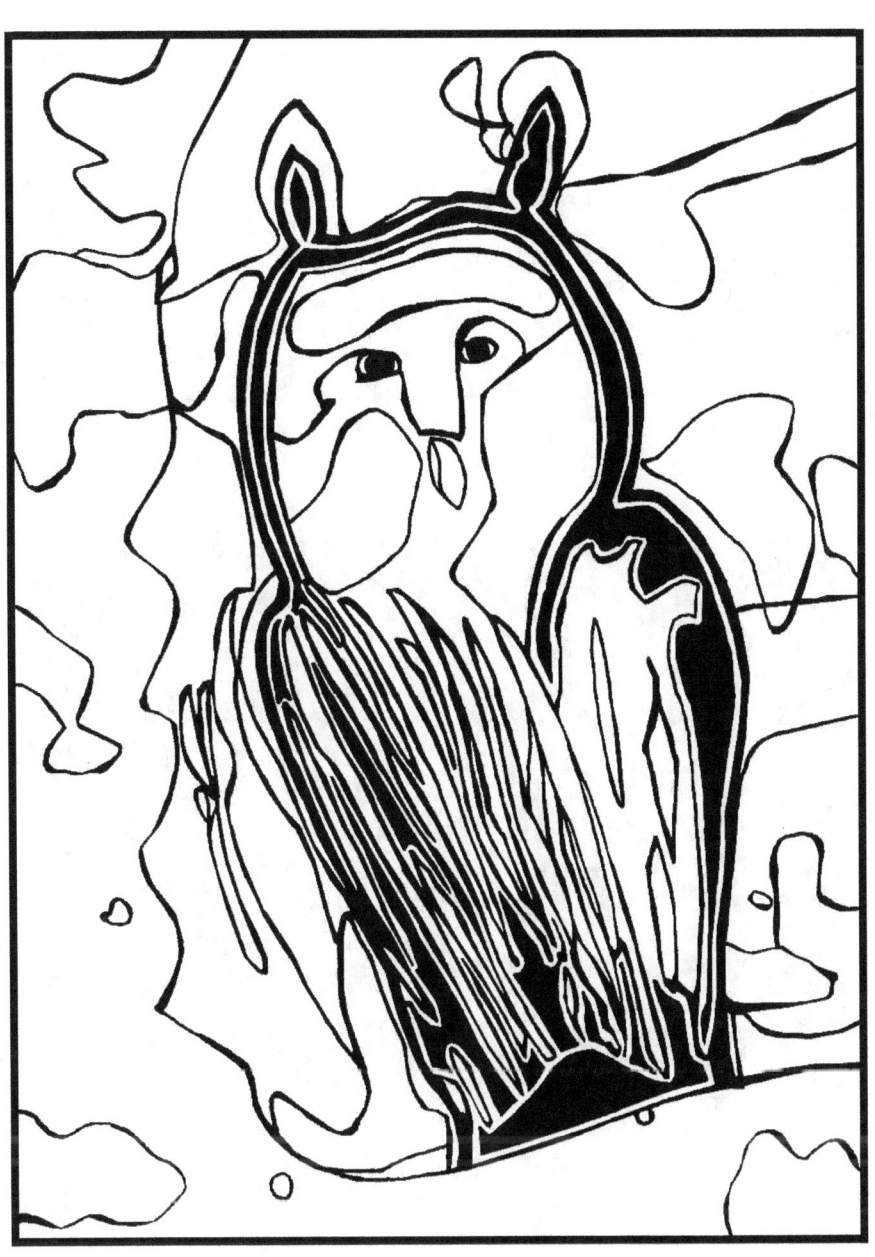

<u>Where it's located</u>: Chauvet-Pont-d'Arc, France

<u>When it was made</u>: Between 36,000 and 30,000 BCE

<u>Why I chose it</u>: I loved how much was going on in this war scene. The men on horseback are a timeless depiction of this world's history.

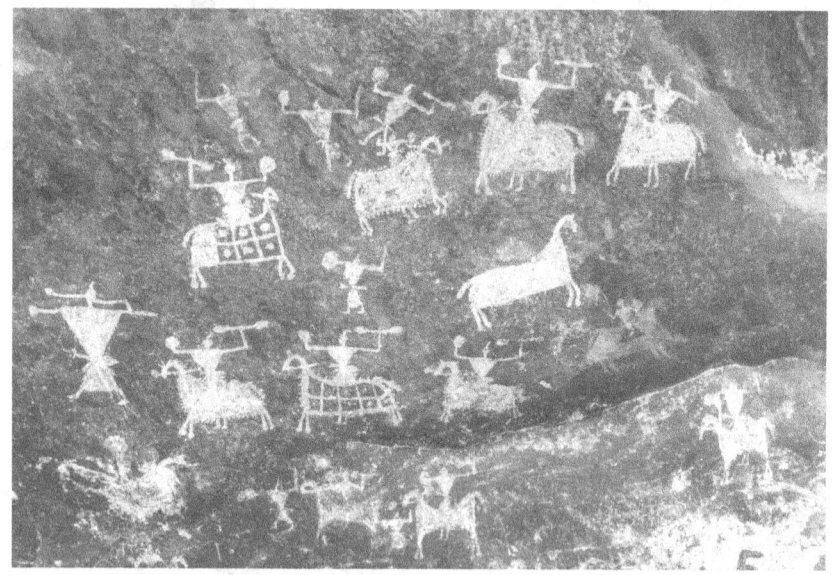

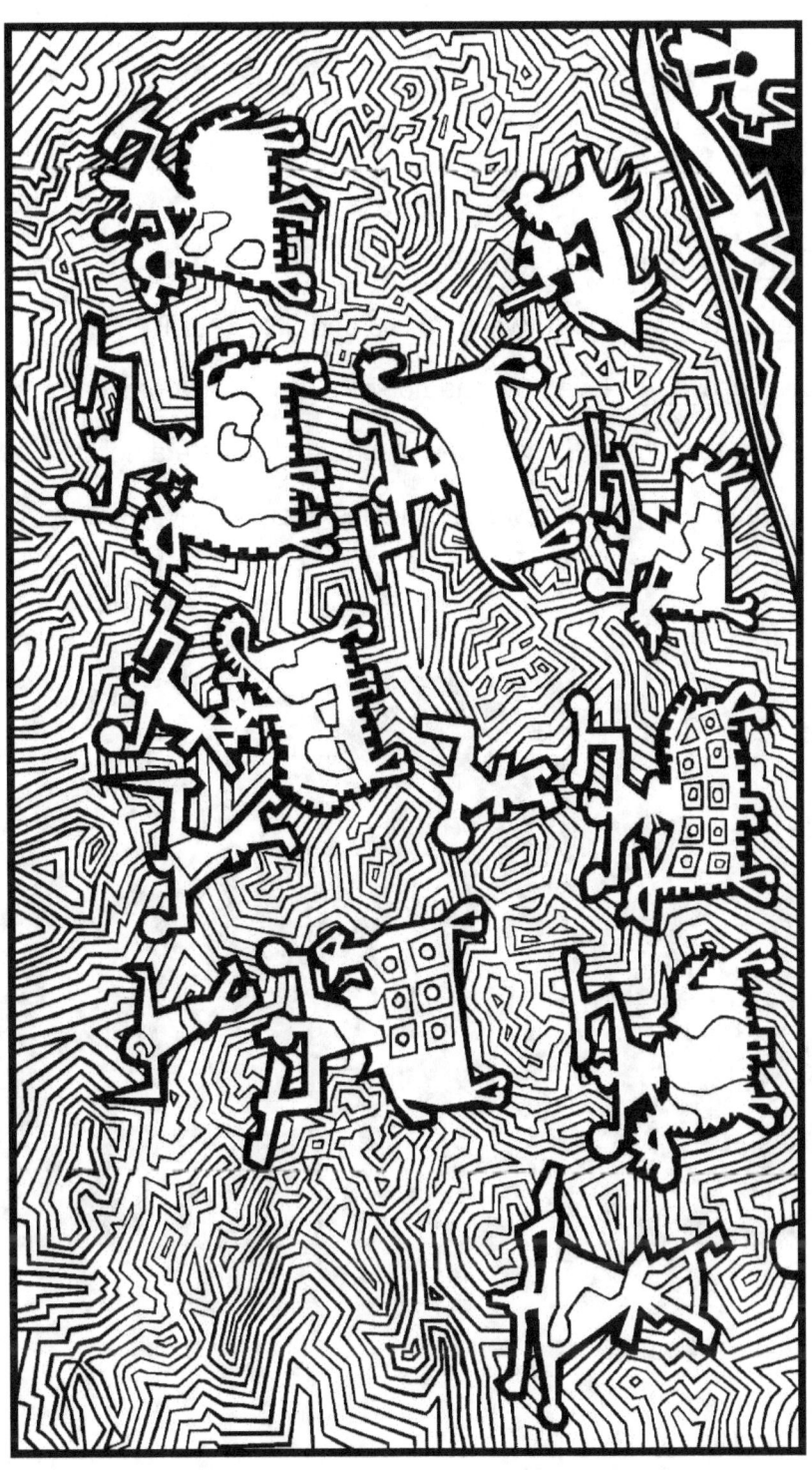

Where it's located: Chauvet-Pont-d'Arc, France

When it was made: Between 36,000 and 30,000 BCE

Why I chose it: I love how the horses and bulls overlap each other in this scene. It has been a source of debate among scholars because it throws their ideals about art evolution on it's head.

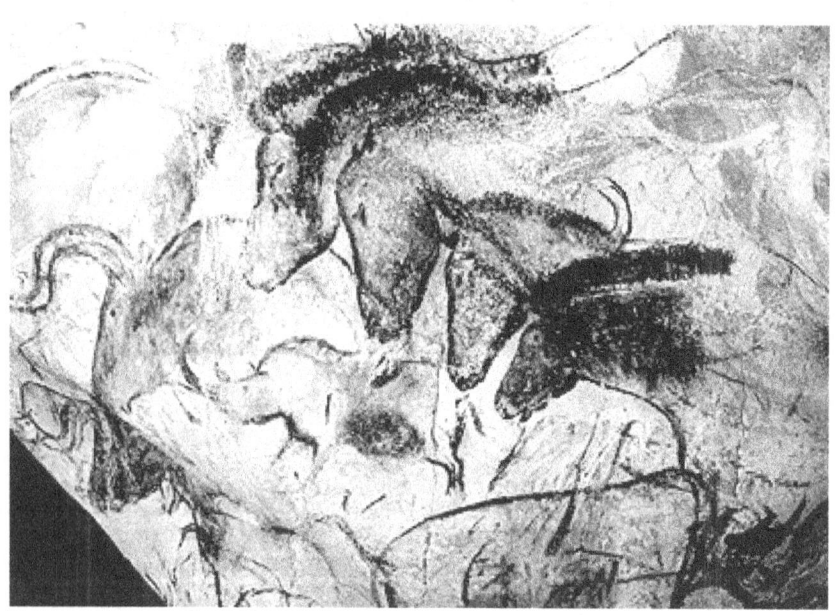

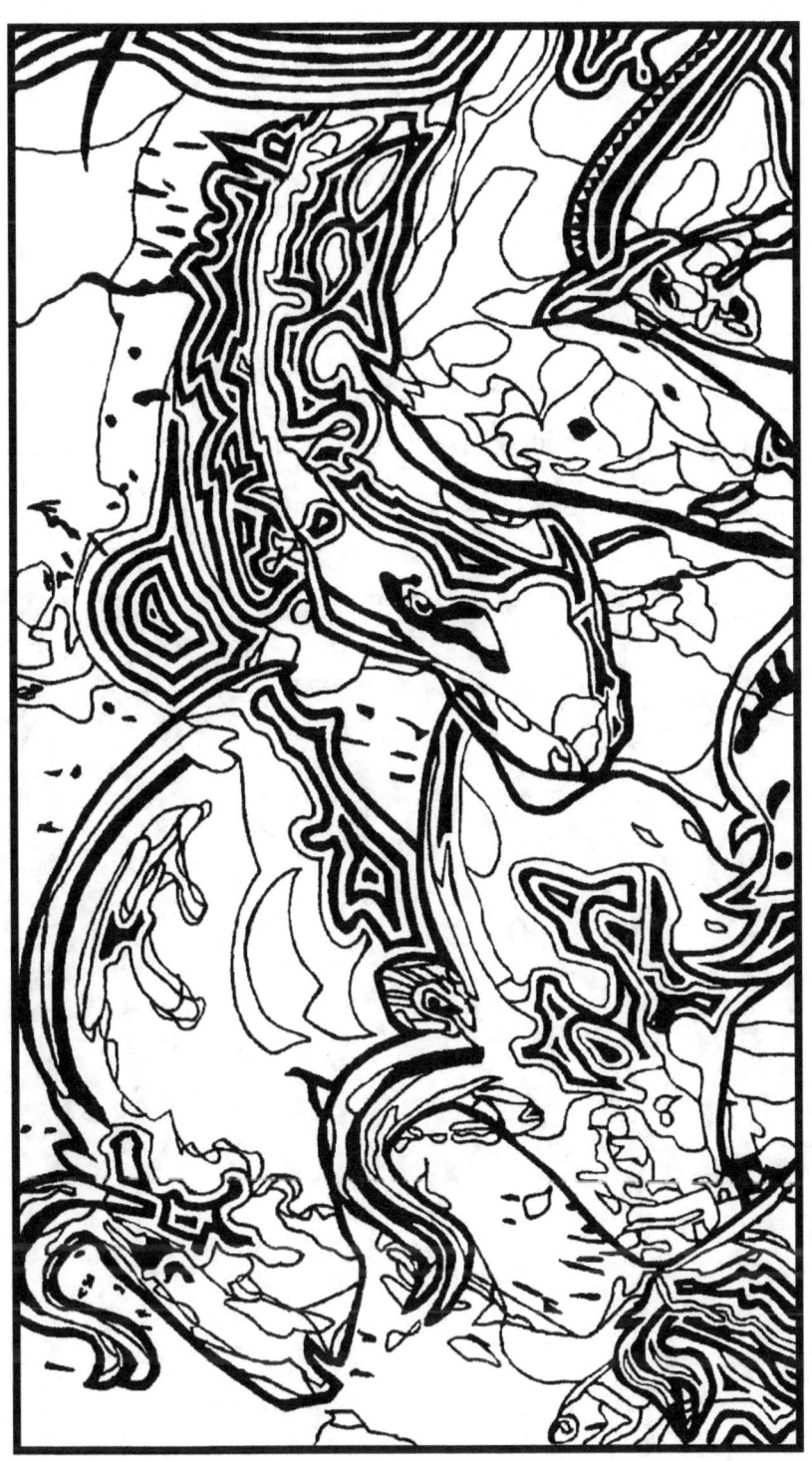

Where it's located: Chauvet-Pont-d'Arc, France

When it was made: Between 36,000 and 30,000 BCE

Why I chose it: I just love this rhinoceros. It gives variety to the menagerie of animals usually seen in cave art.

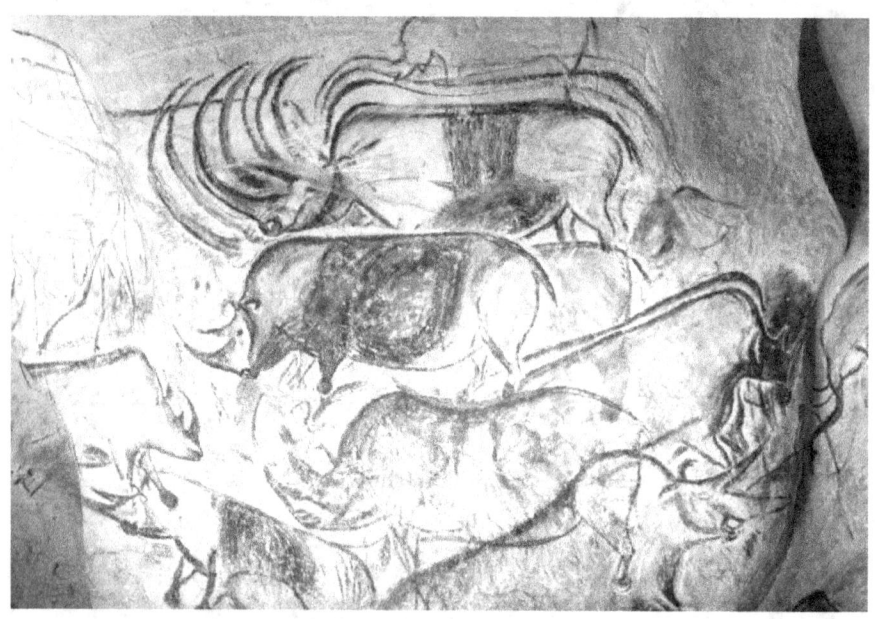

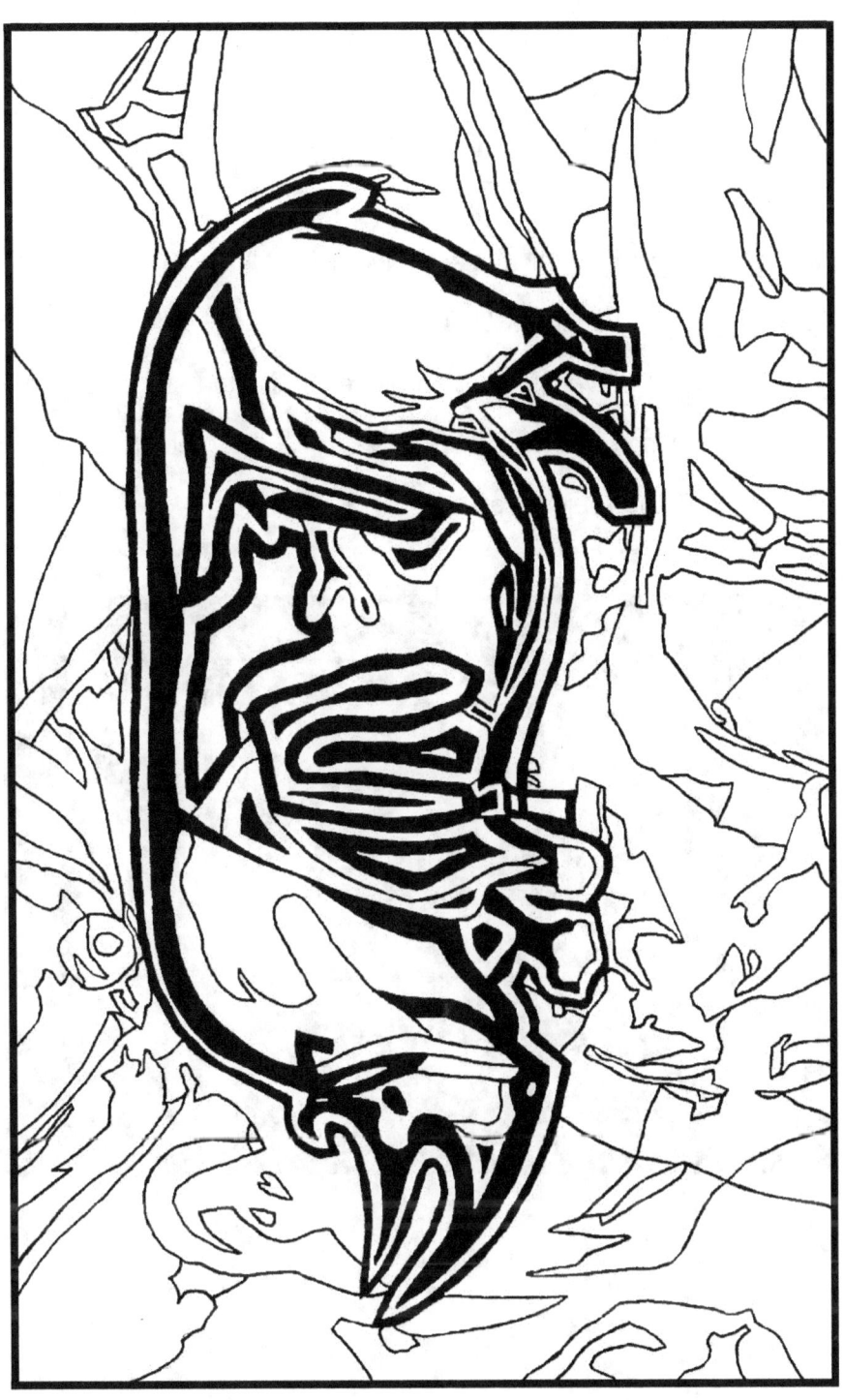

<u>Where it's located:</u> Pech Merle, France

<u>When it was made:</u> About 25,000 BCE

<u>Why I chose it:</u> I love the spotted horses and hand signatures in this cave. For me, the hands bring reality to the prehistoric world in a way no other object can.

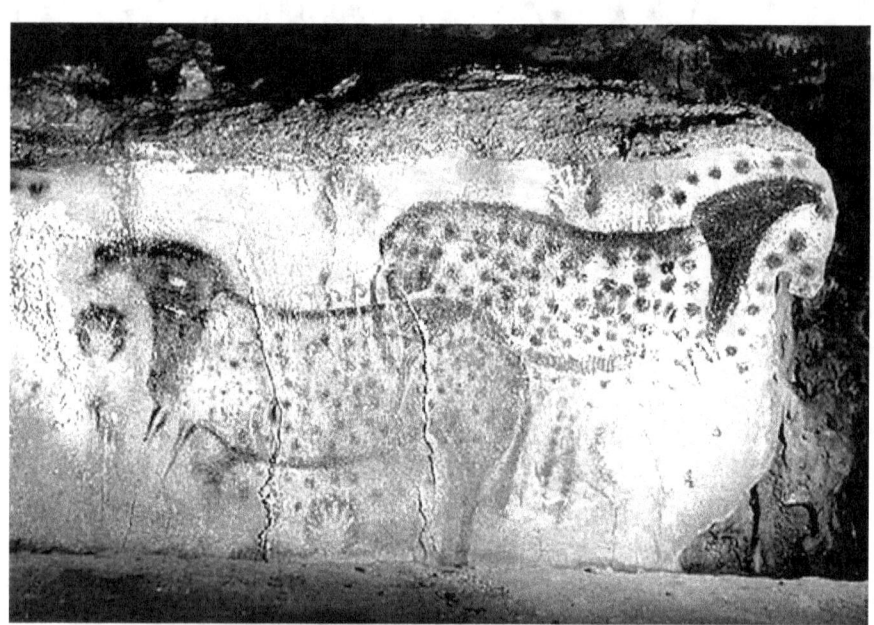

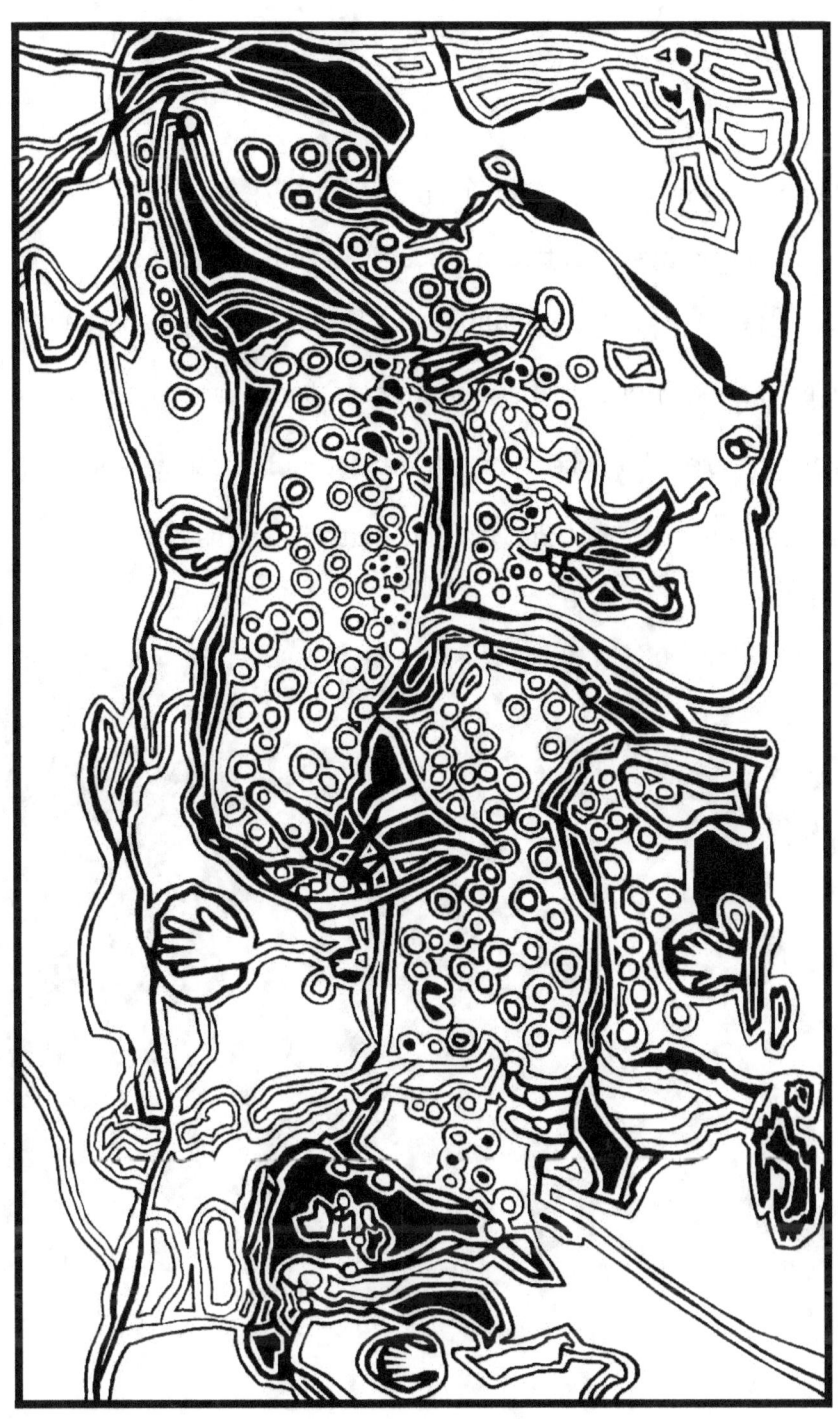

Where it's located: Val Camonica, Italy

When it was made: Between 8,000 BCE and 1,000 AD

Why I chose it: These carvings have been made for thousands of

years and each one give a unique insight into prehistoric life.

Many people who believe in extraterrestrial life believe these

carvings are proof of them visiting Earth in prehistoric times

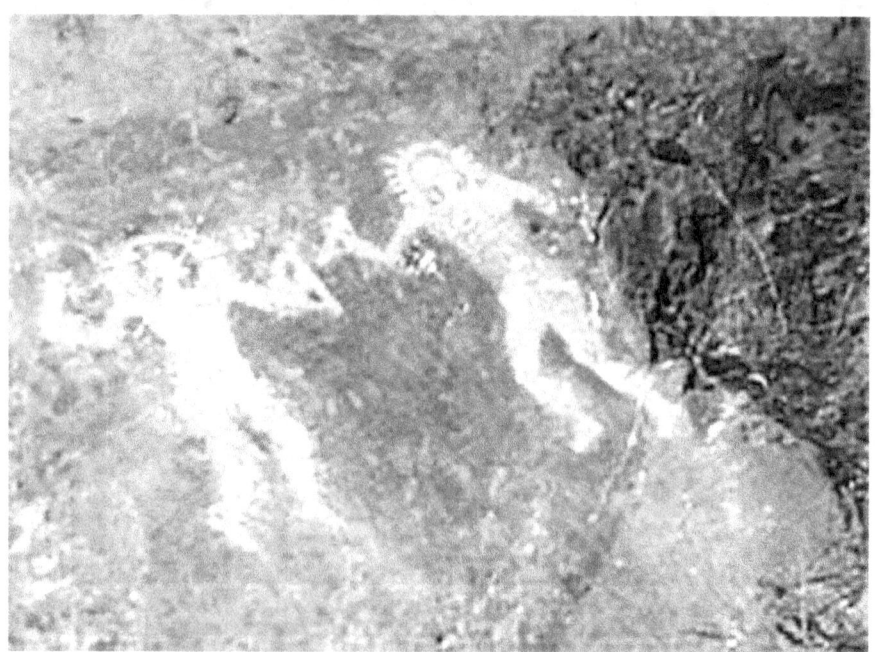

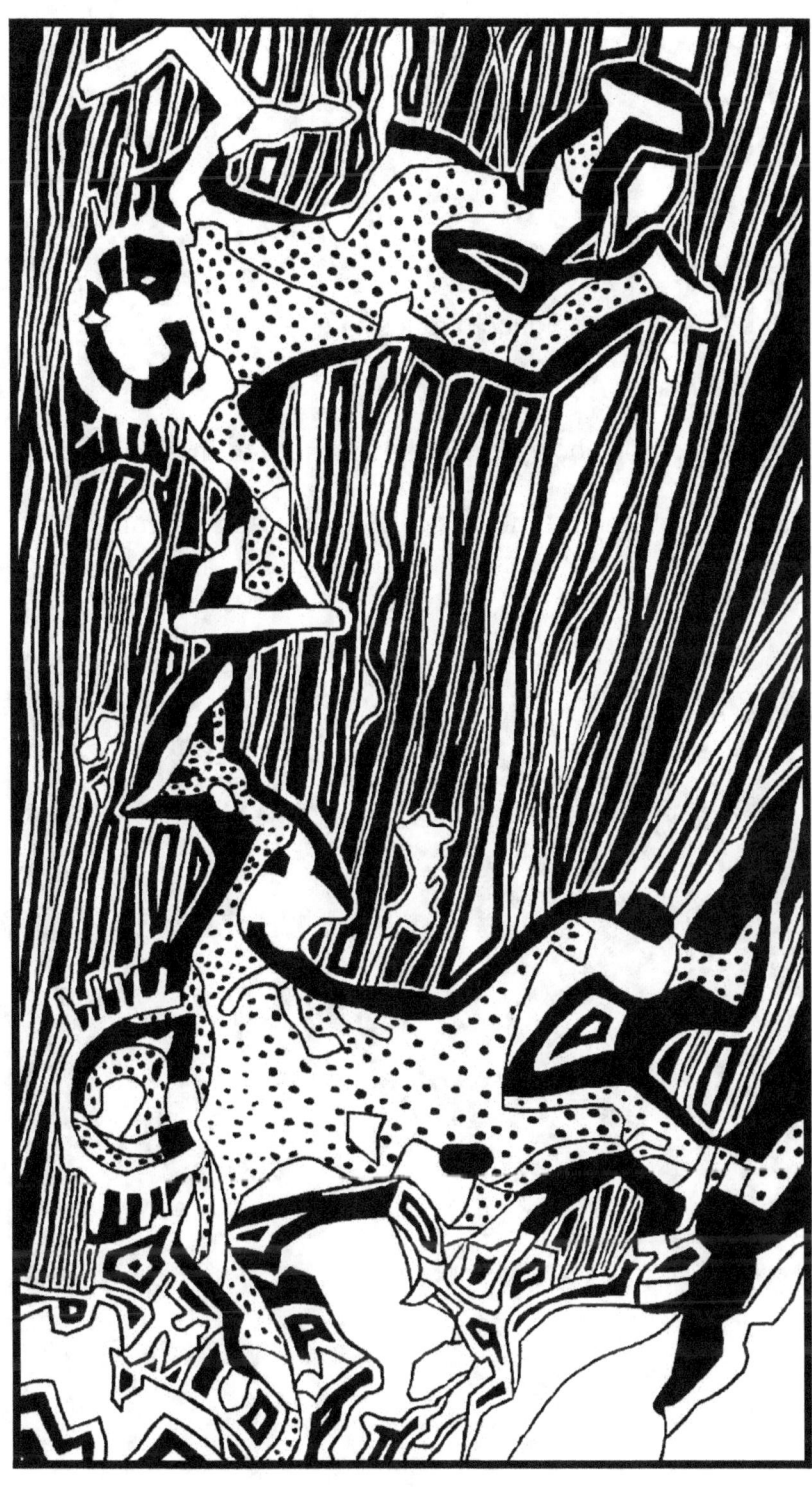

Where it's located: Rouffignac, France

When it was made: About 11,000 BCE

Why I chose it: I love how simple the lines are in these animal

drawings. It gives me a thrill to see the bison and the rams

mixed together.

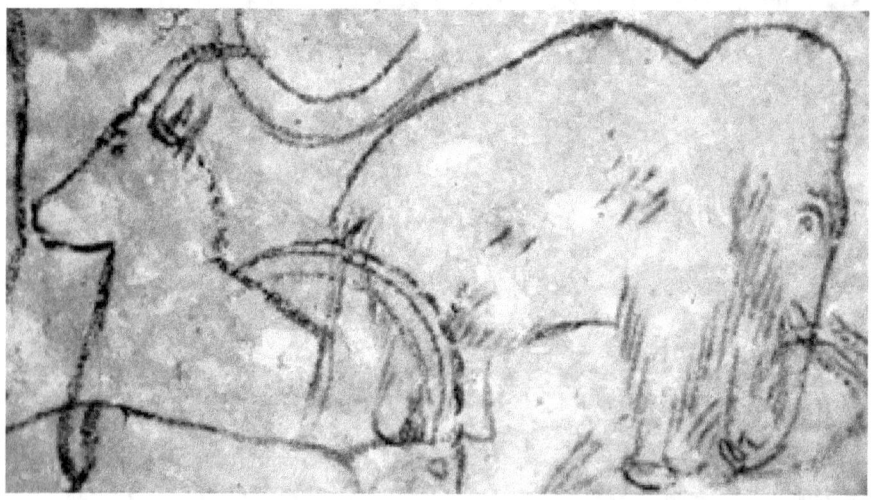

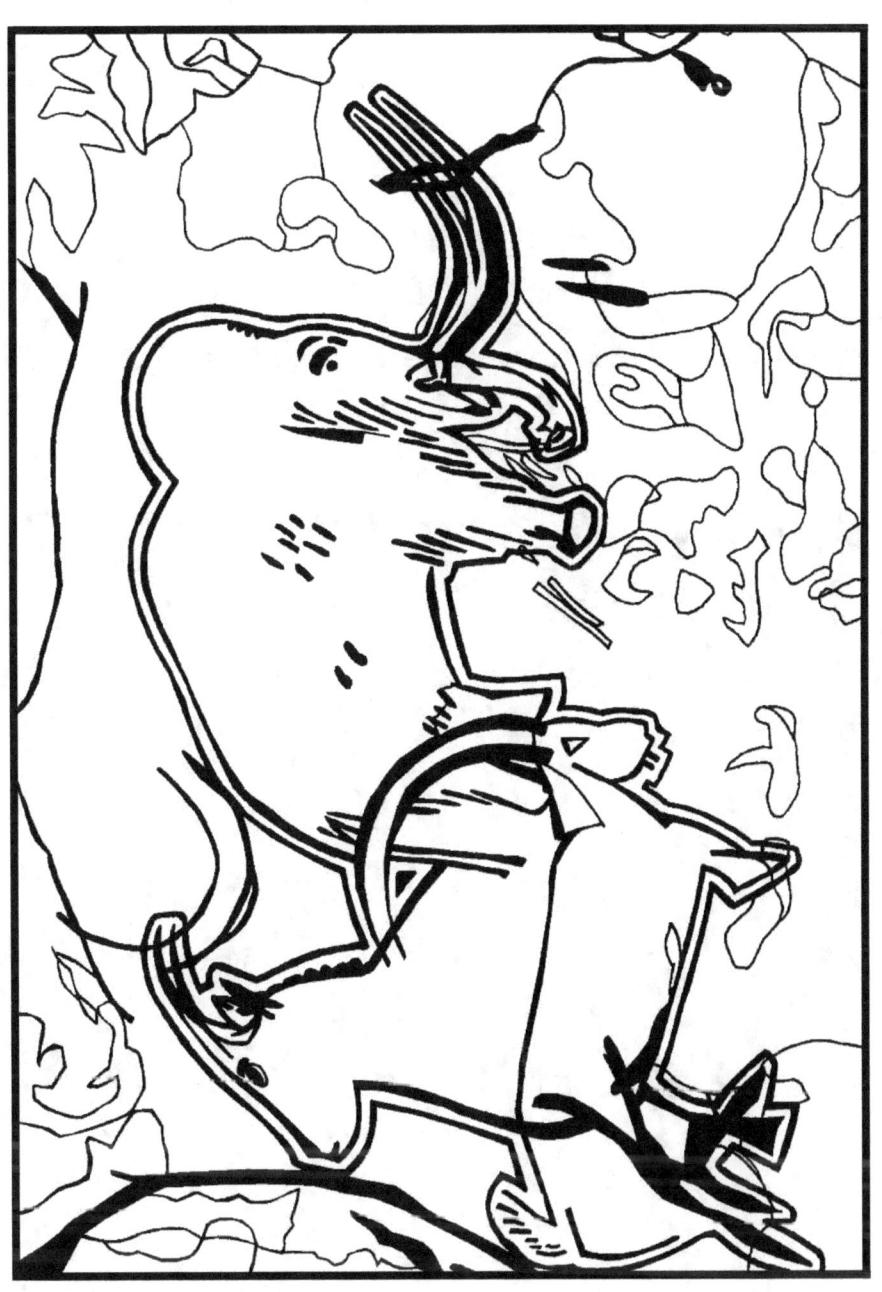

Where it's located: Rouffignac, France

When it was made: About 11,000 BCE

Why I chose it: To me these simple lines just scream, "Draw me! Color me!" and I had to listen.

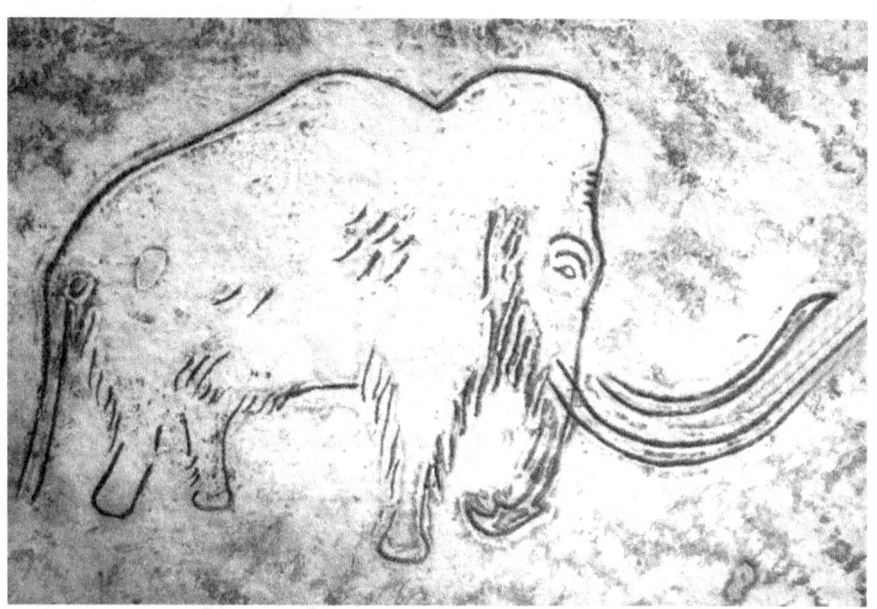

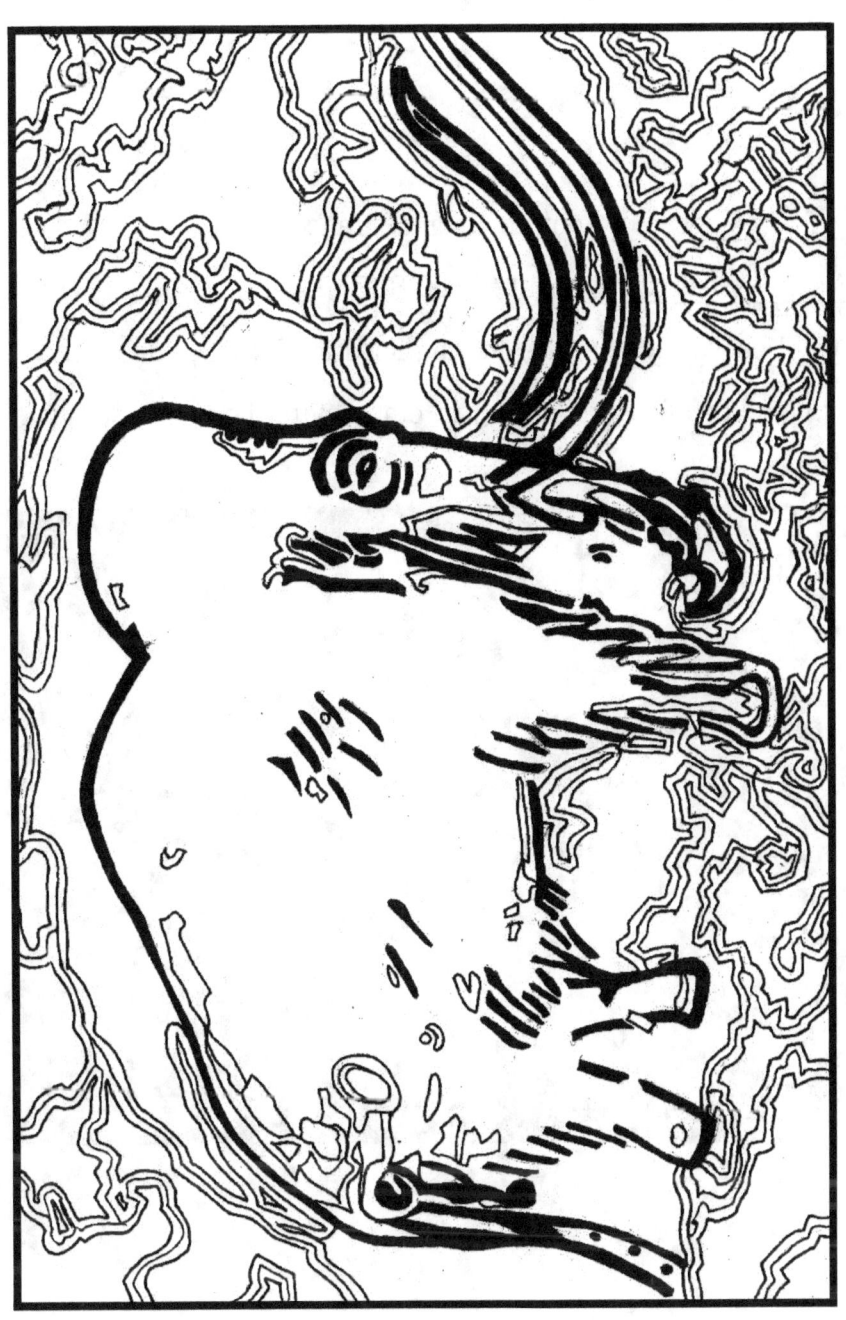

Where it's located: Font-de-Gaume, France

When it was made: About 25,000 BCE

Why I chose it: I love the curving lines on these reindeer. The curving lines flow and help give empathy to the wounded deer.

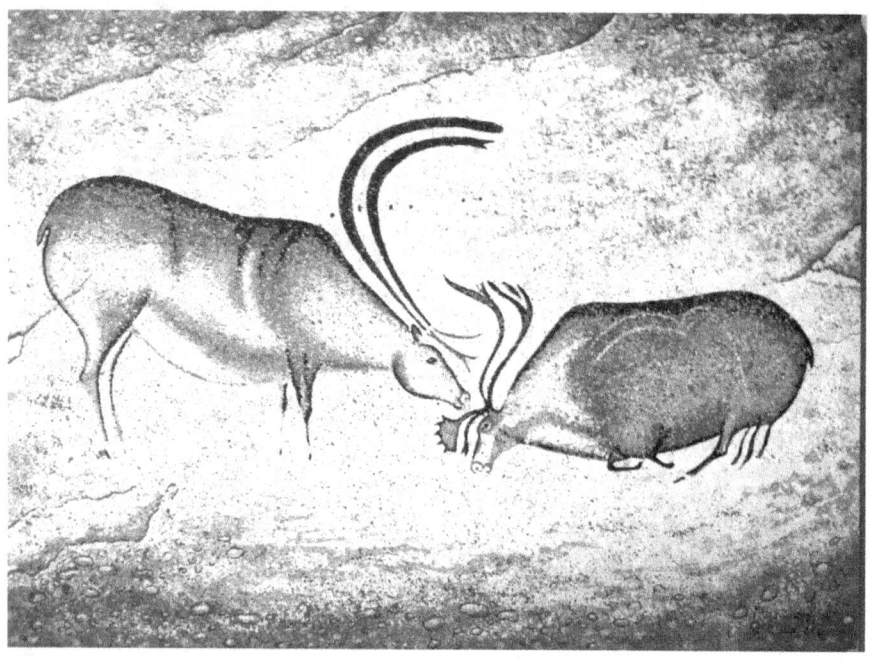

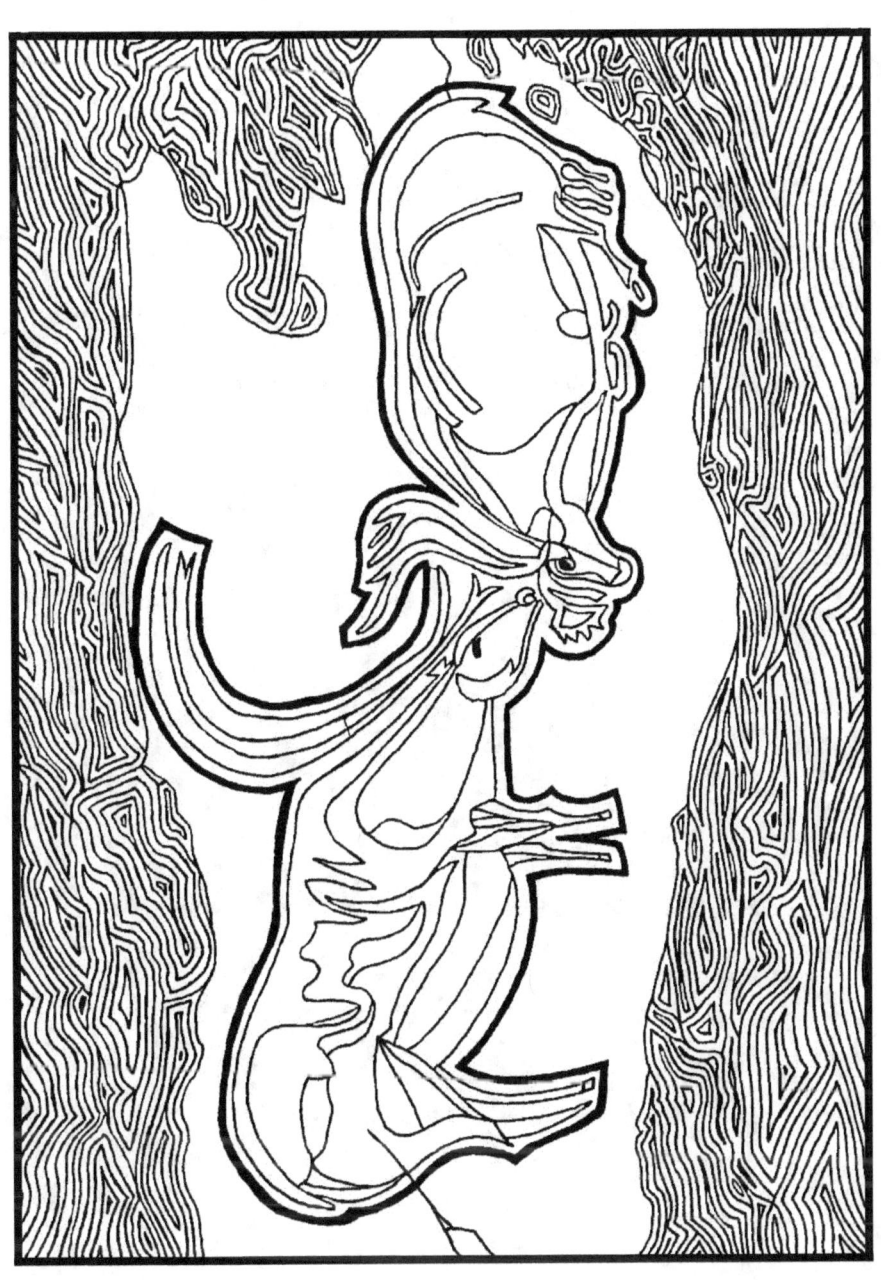

Where it's located: Serra da Capivara, Brazil

When it was made: About 23,000 BCE

Why I chose it: I love to look at art on a global scale. Cave art is not only found in Eurasia but on every continent.

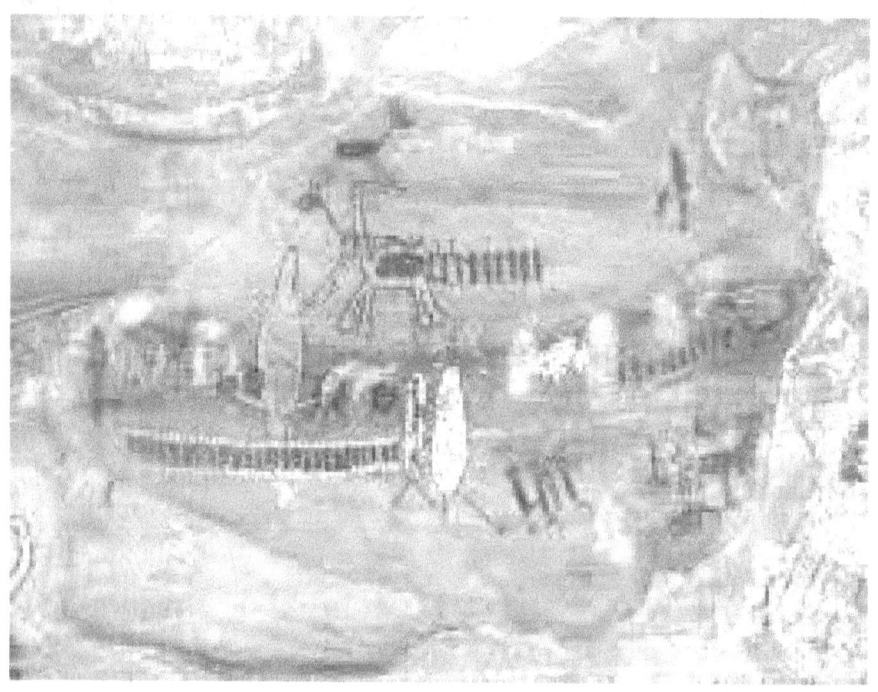

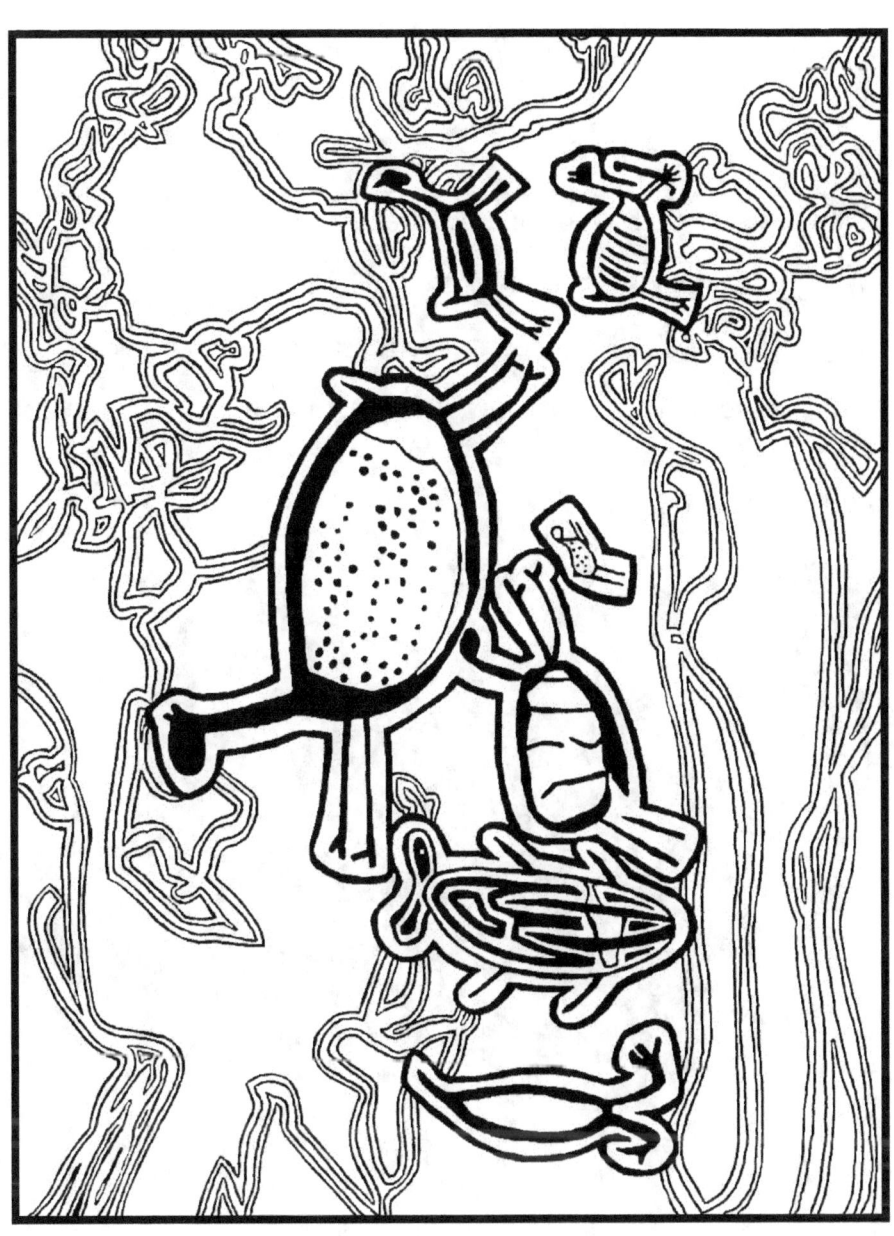

<u>Where it's located:</u> Wandijina, Australia

<u>When it was made:</u> Dates back to 3,000 BCE

<u>Why I chose it:</u> The large eyes give these figures an other-worldly appearance. I have always been captivated by their alien stare.

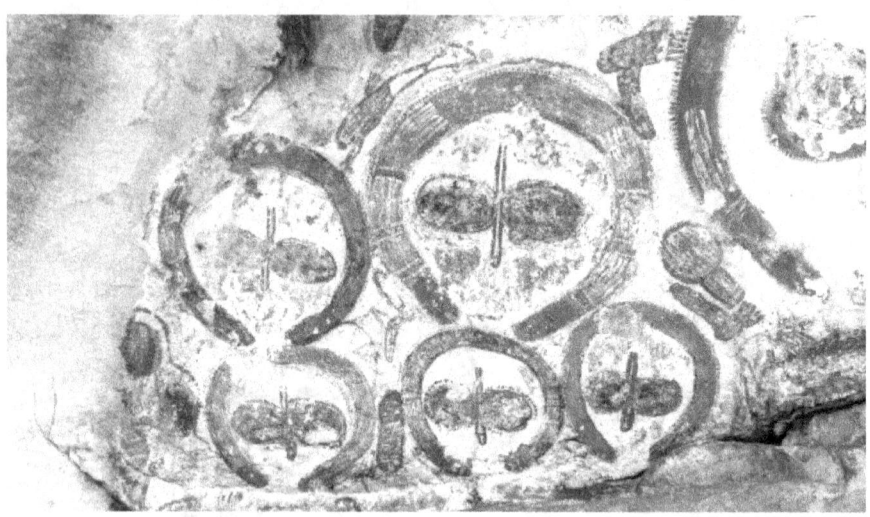

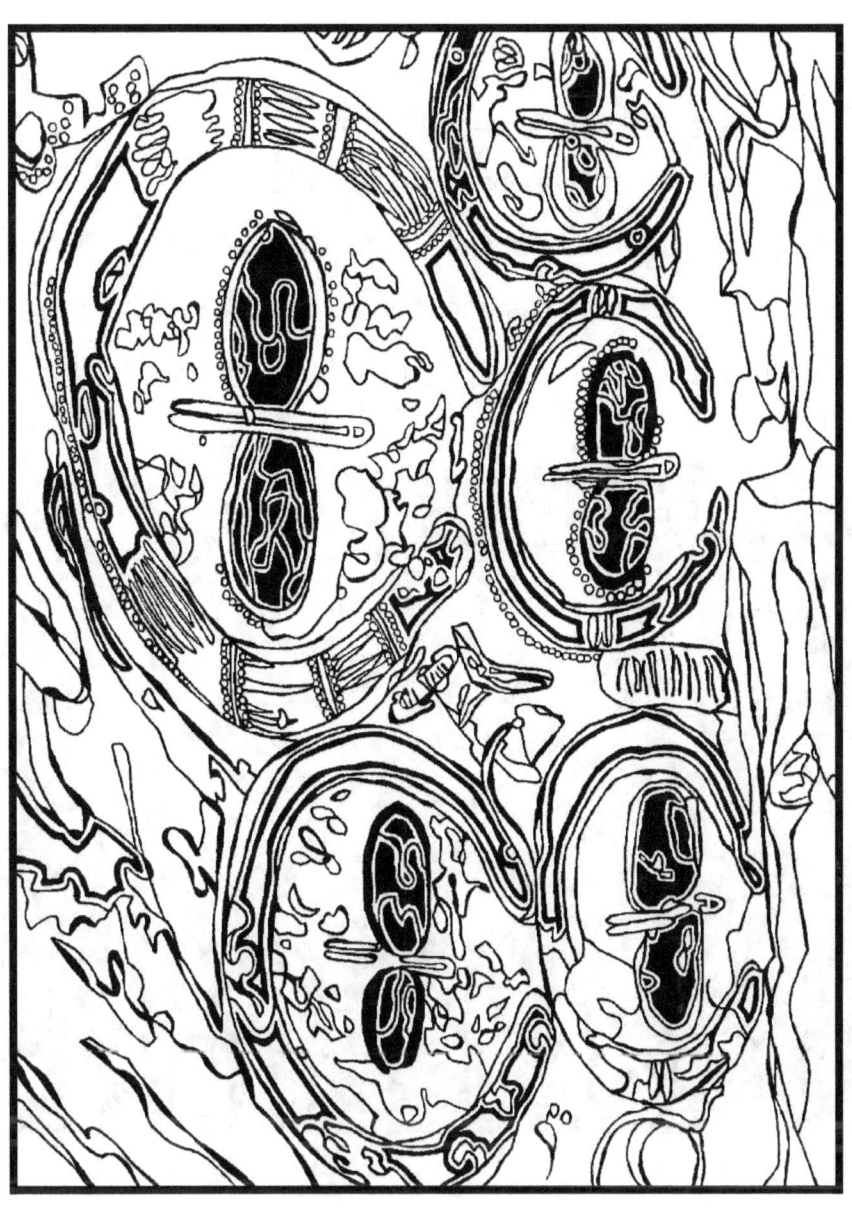

Where it's located: Wandijina, Australia

When it was made: Dates back to 3,000 BCE

Why I chose it: I'm almost afraid of the story behind this painting. I'm not a fan of snakes and meeting one that large is something that will feature in my nightmares for years to come.

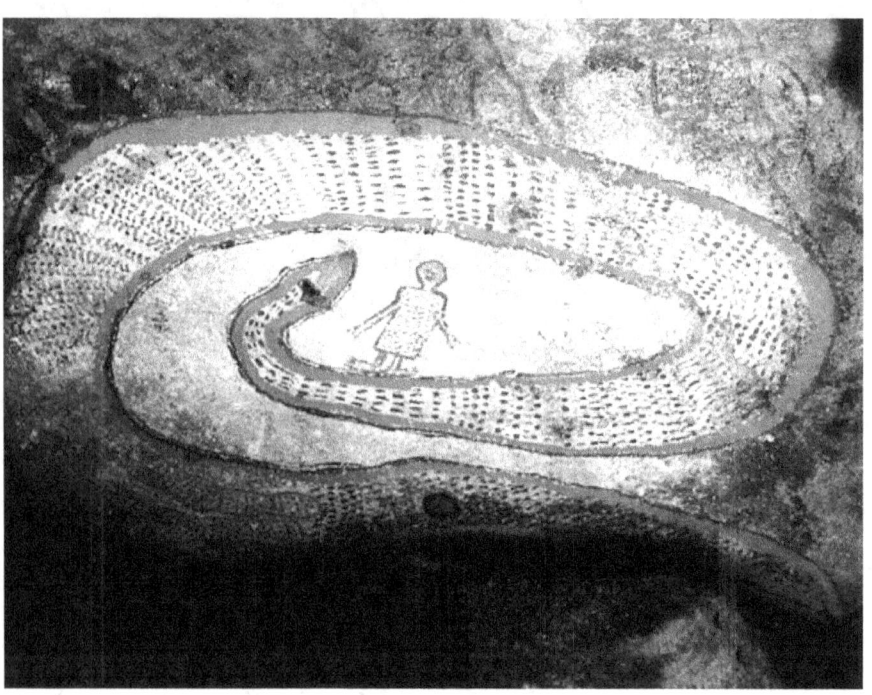

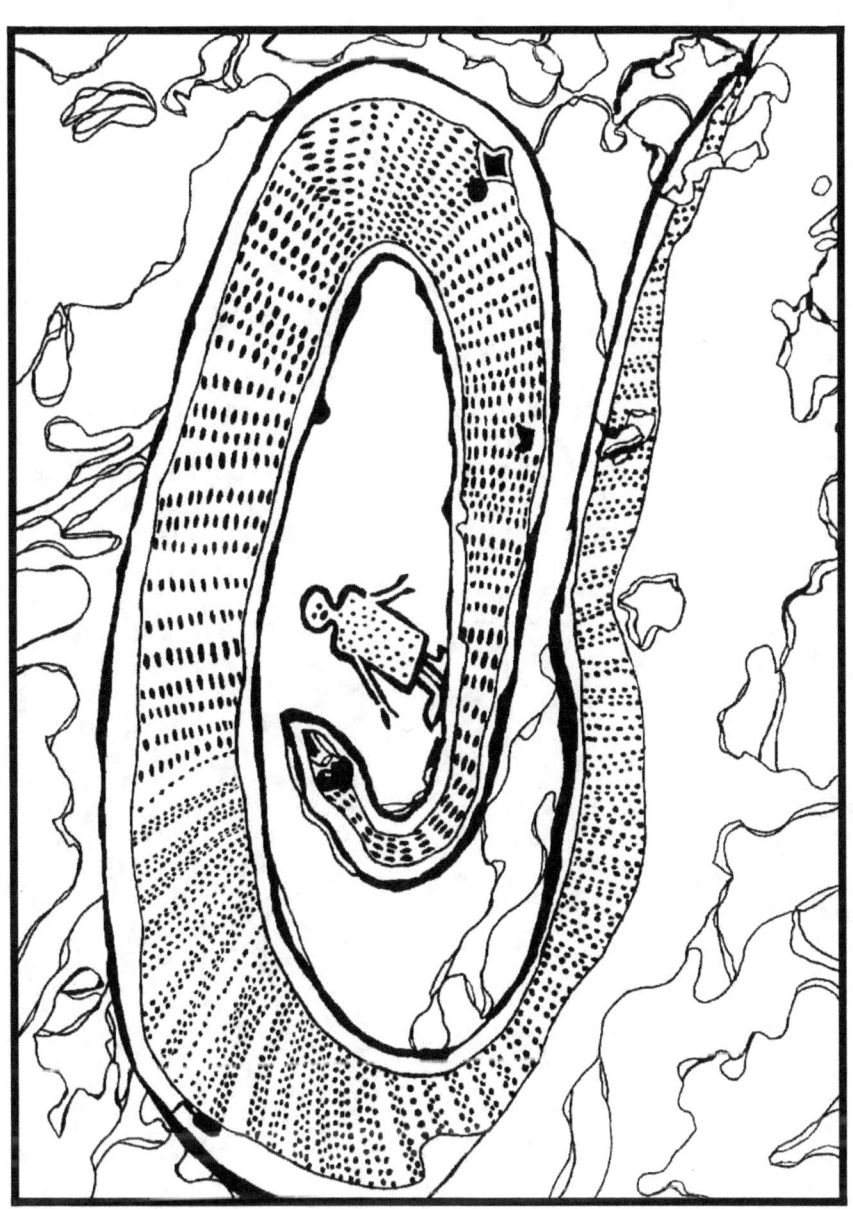

Where it's located: Tassili-n-Ajjer, Algeria

When it was made: About 8,000 BCE

Why I chose it: I just love giraffes and jumped at the chance of creating a unique piece of art based on these cave paintings.

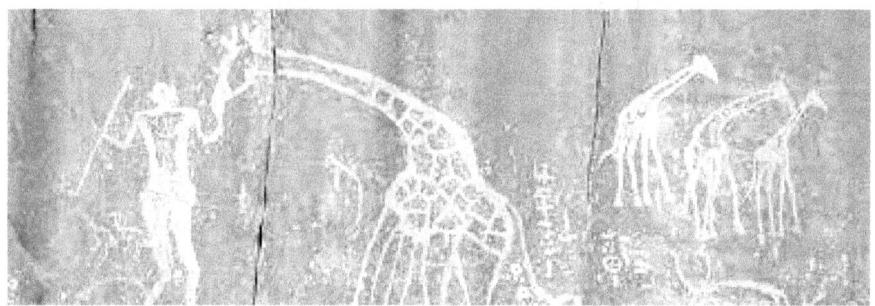

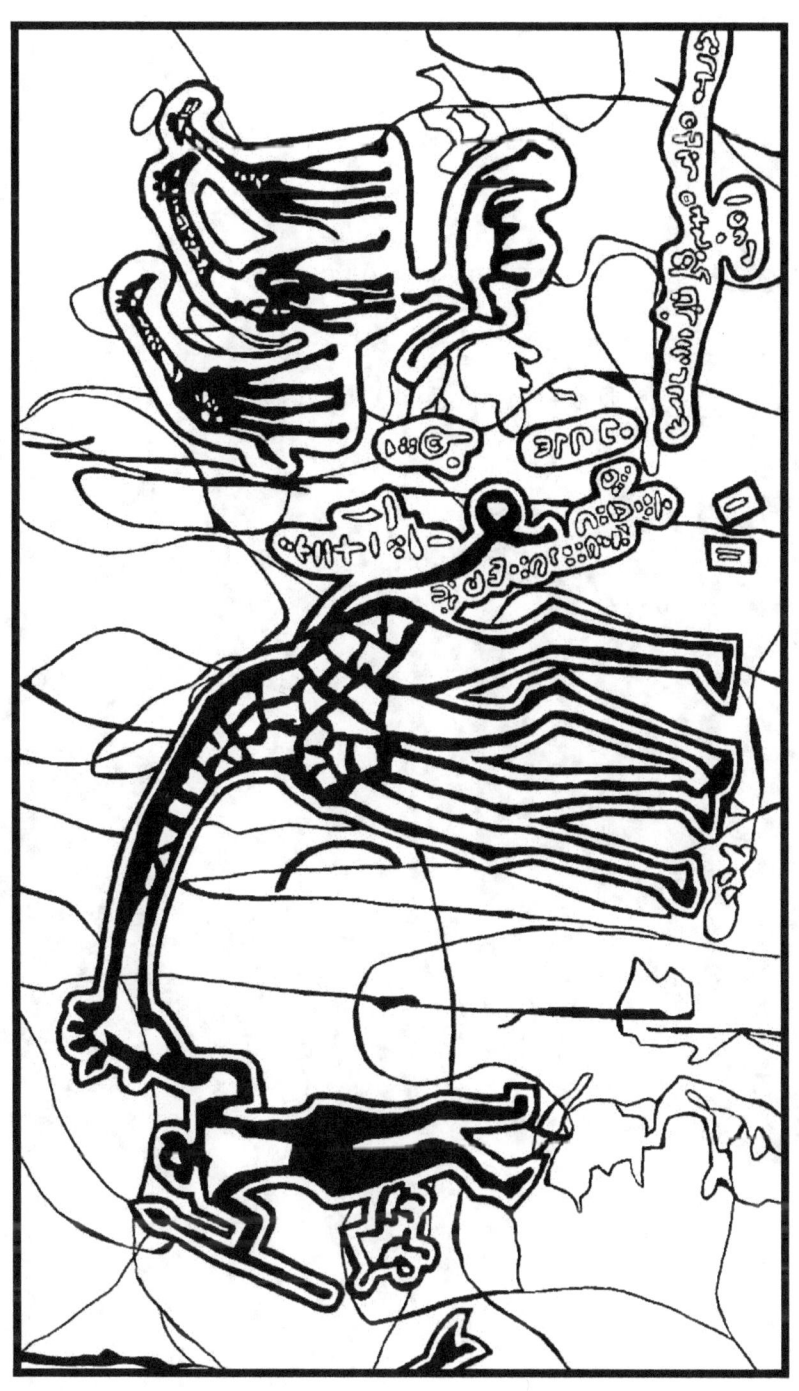

Where it's located: Tassili-n-Ajjer, Algeria

When it was made: About 8,000 BCE

Why I chose it: They are giraffes! Why not?!

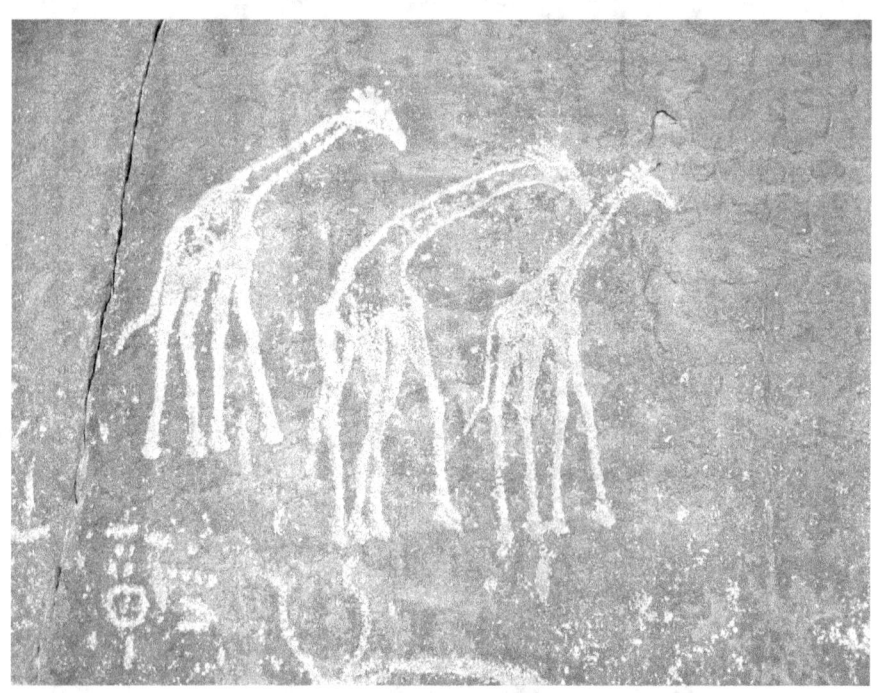

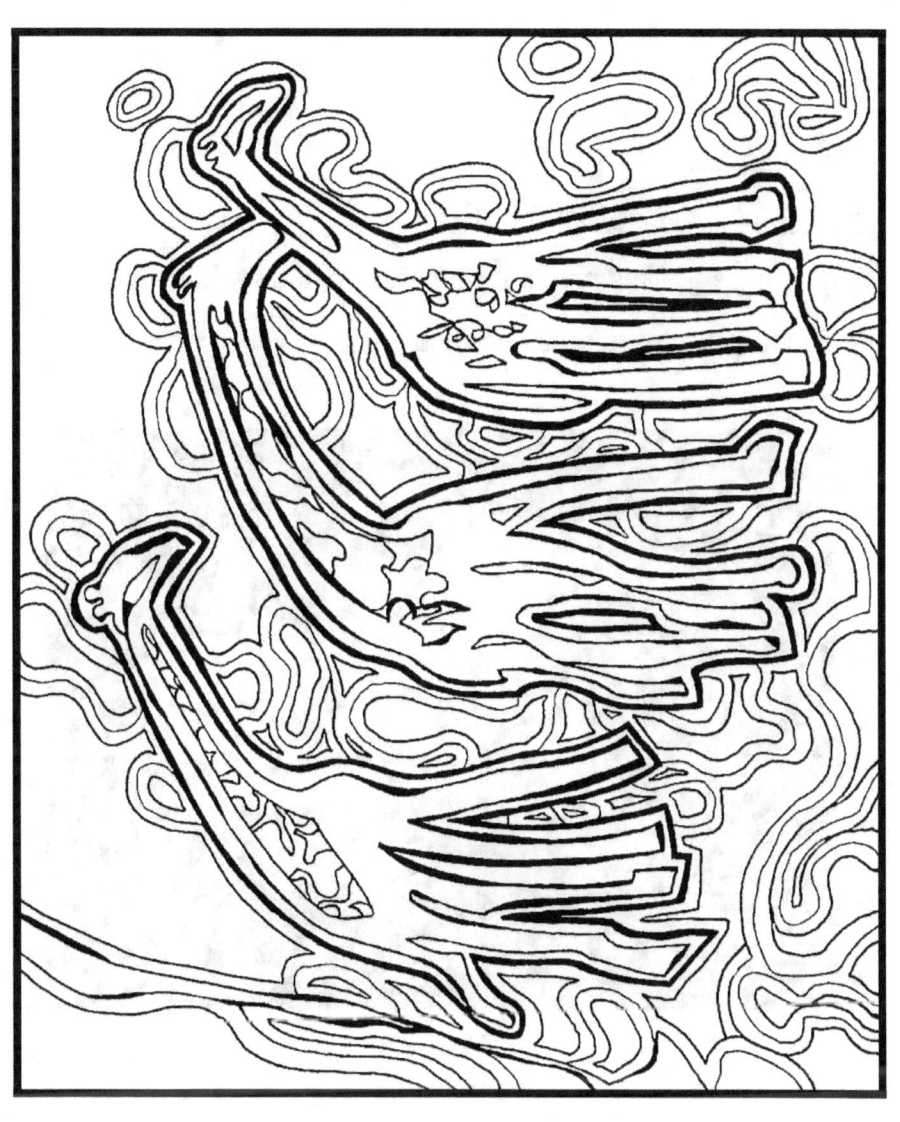

<u>Where it's located:</u> France

<u>When it was made:</u> 12,000 BCE

<u>Why I chose it:</u> This may not be a cave painting, but I love the detail carved into this reindeer horn.

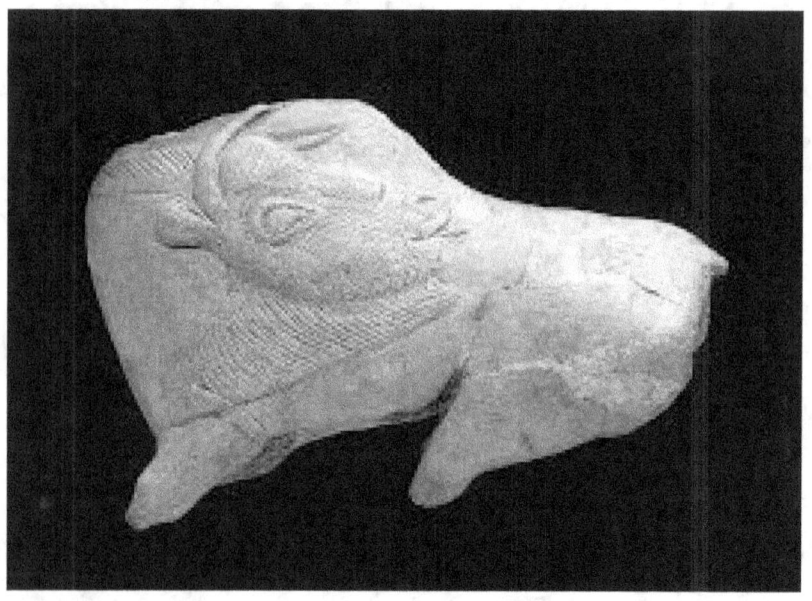

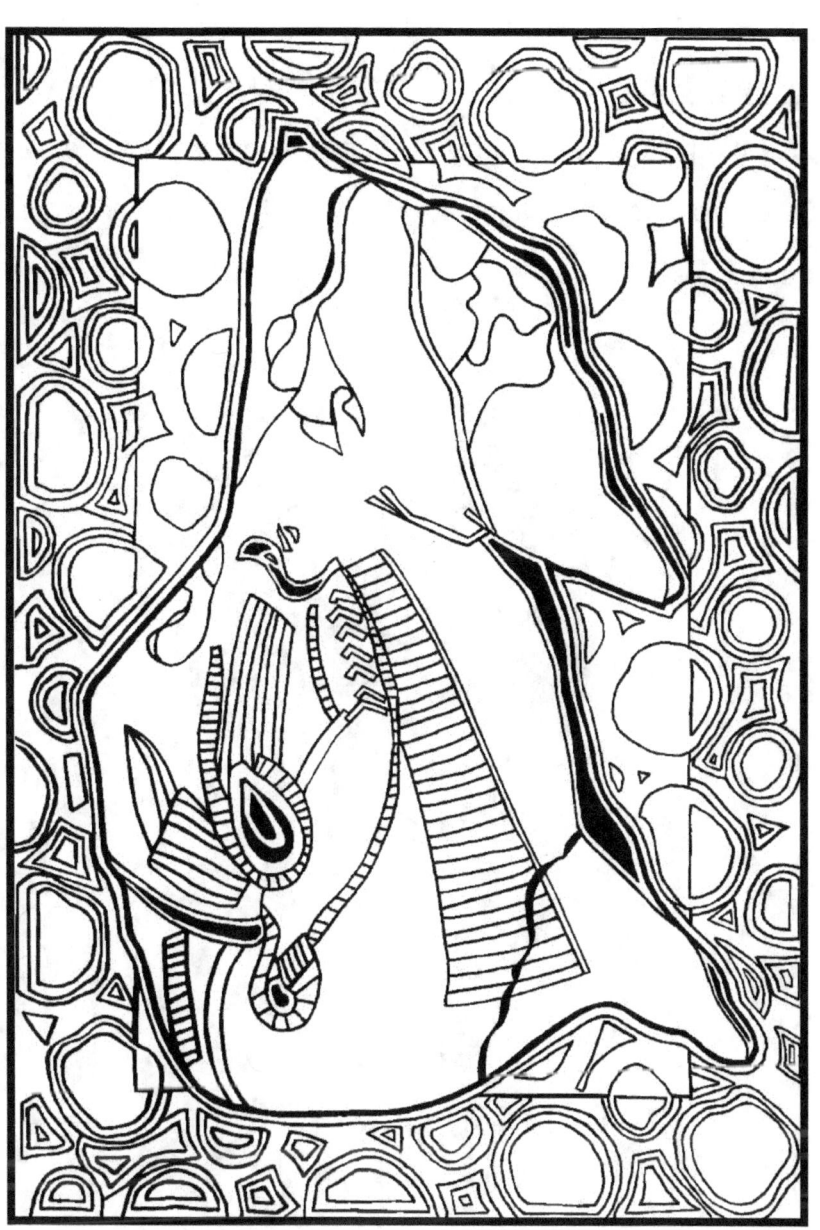

<u>Where it's located:</u> Trois-Freses, France

<u>When it was made:</u> About 13,000 BCE

<u>Why I chose it:</u> This is one of the most famous "fake" cave paintings there is. The details you can see in my piece are based on the elaborate and exaggerated sketch which is based on an original cave painting.

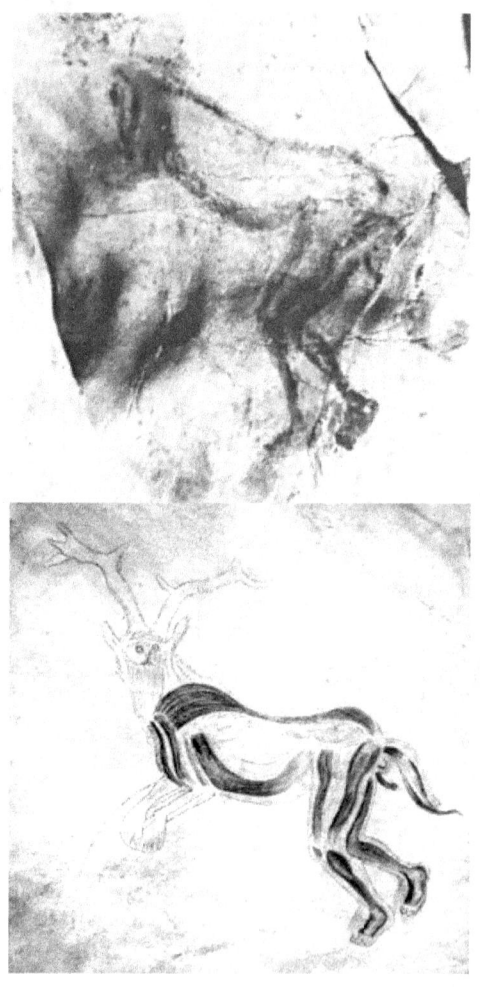

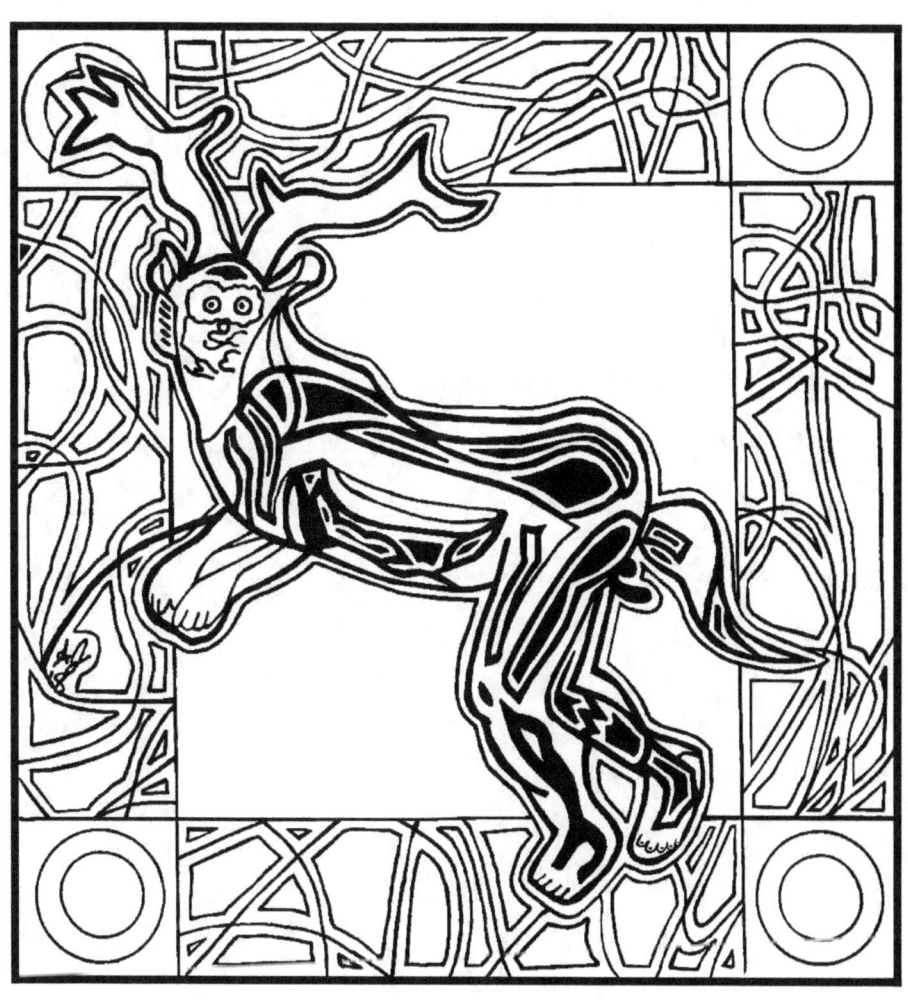

<u>What is it:</u> Cave Painting of Primitive Man by Nomad

<u>Why I chose it:</u> This modern recreation was an inspiration for me as I searched for pieces to recreate. I also loved that my children helped me with some of the random lines you can see running across the page.

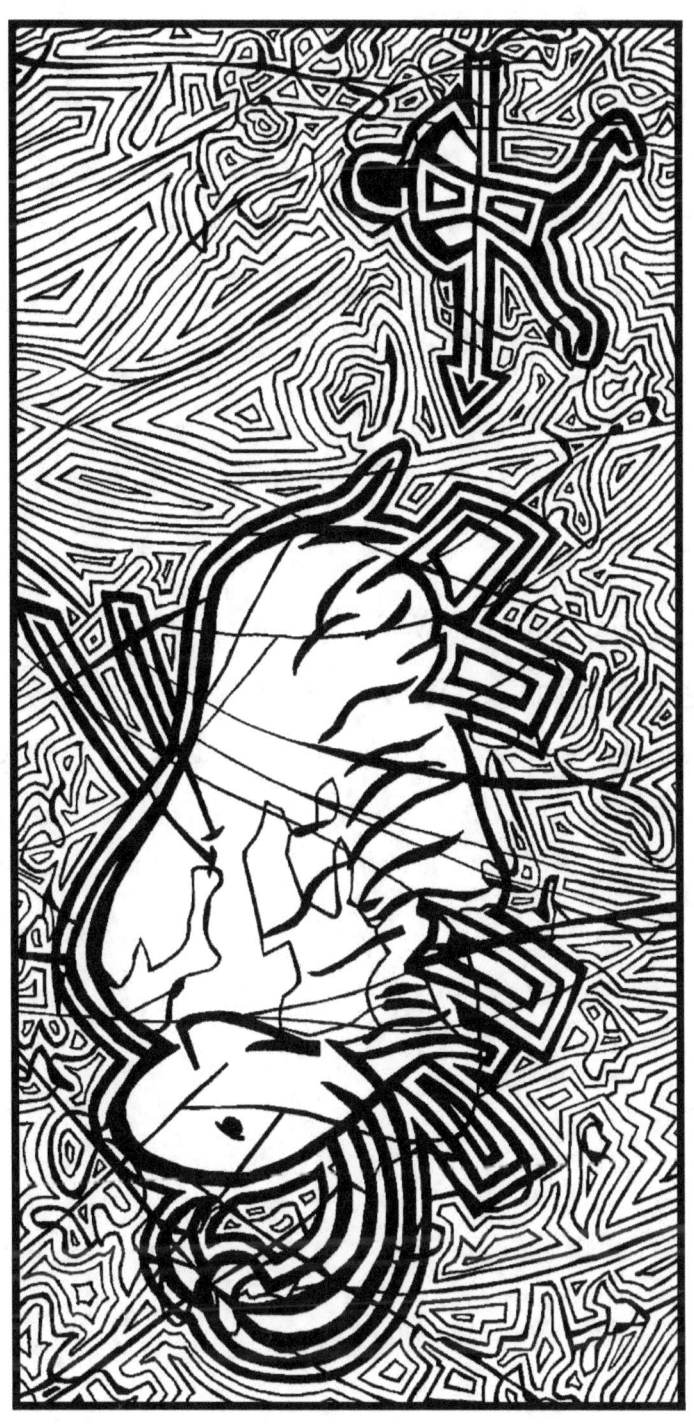

<u>What is it</u>: Hunting Scene With Two Deer

<u>Why I chose it</u>: This is a typical modern "cave painting" recreation. I loved the crisp lines of the hunters and wanted to elaborate on that.

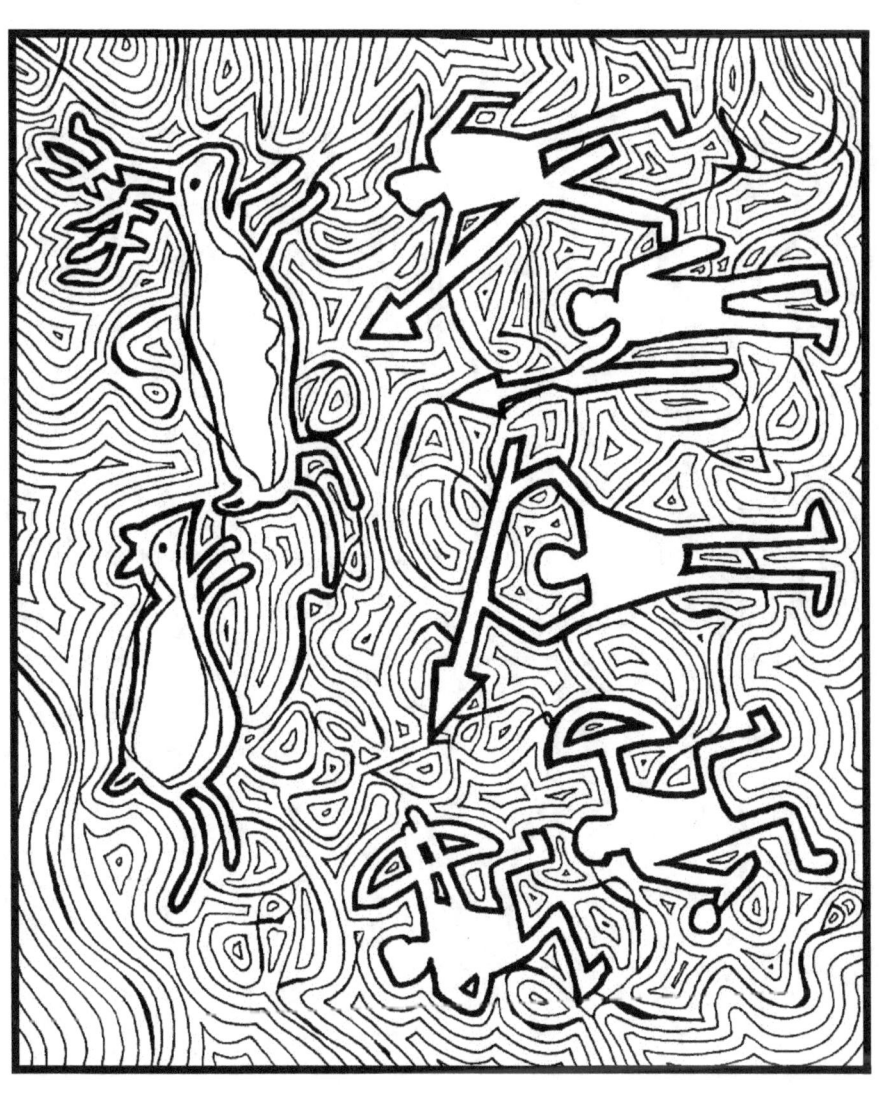

<u>What is it:</u> Two Hedgehogs

<u>Why I chose it:</u> I love hedgehogs and this playful interpretation of a cave painting just made me smile.

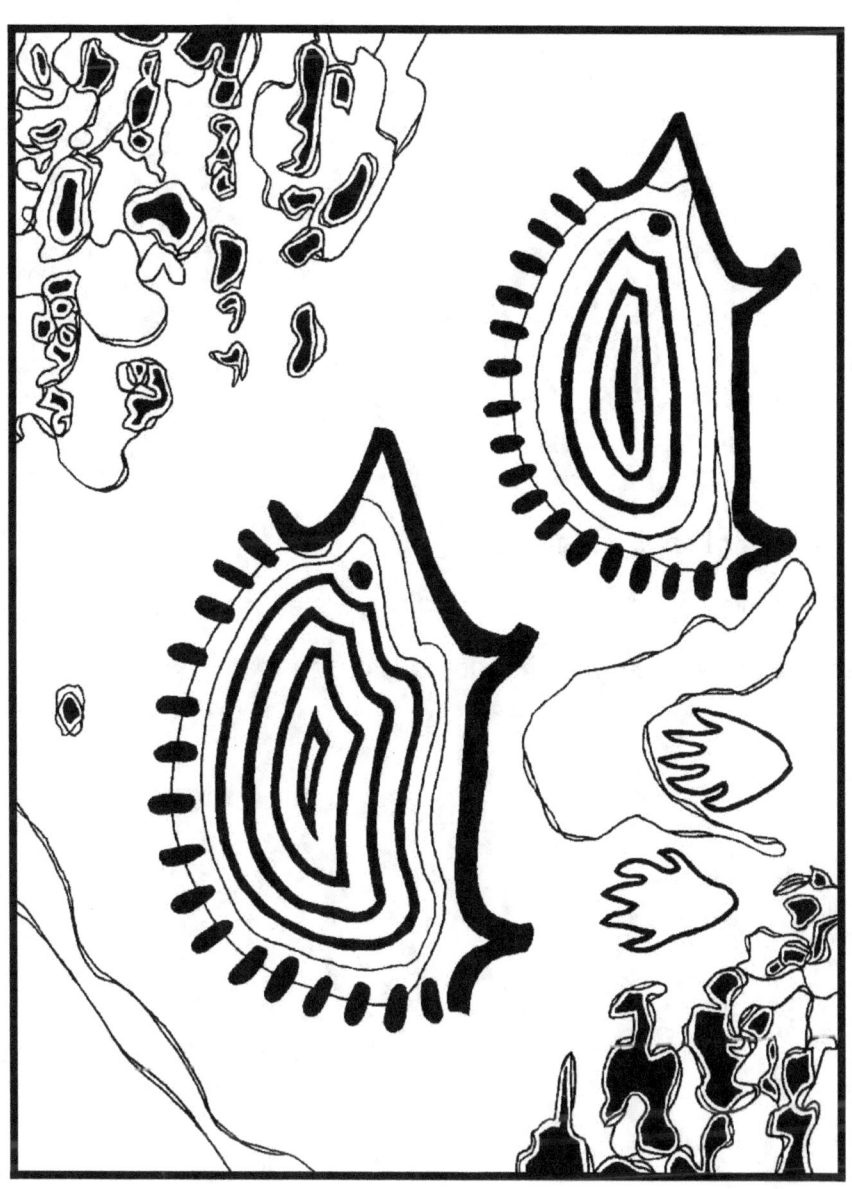

<u>What is it:</u> Ibex Hunt in Spain

<u>Why I chose it:</u> The skeletal hunter intrigued me. It may not be a true cave painting, but that doesn't mean it can be inspiring.

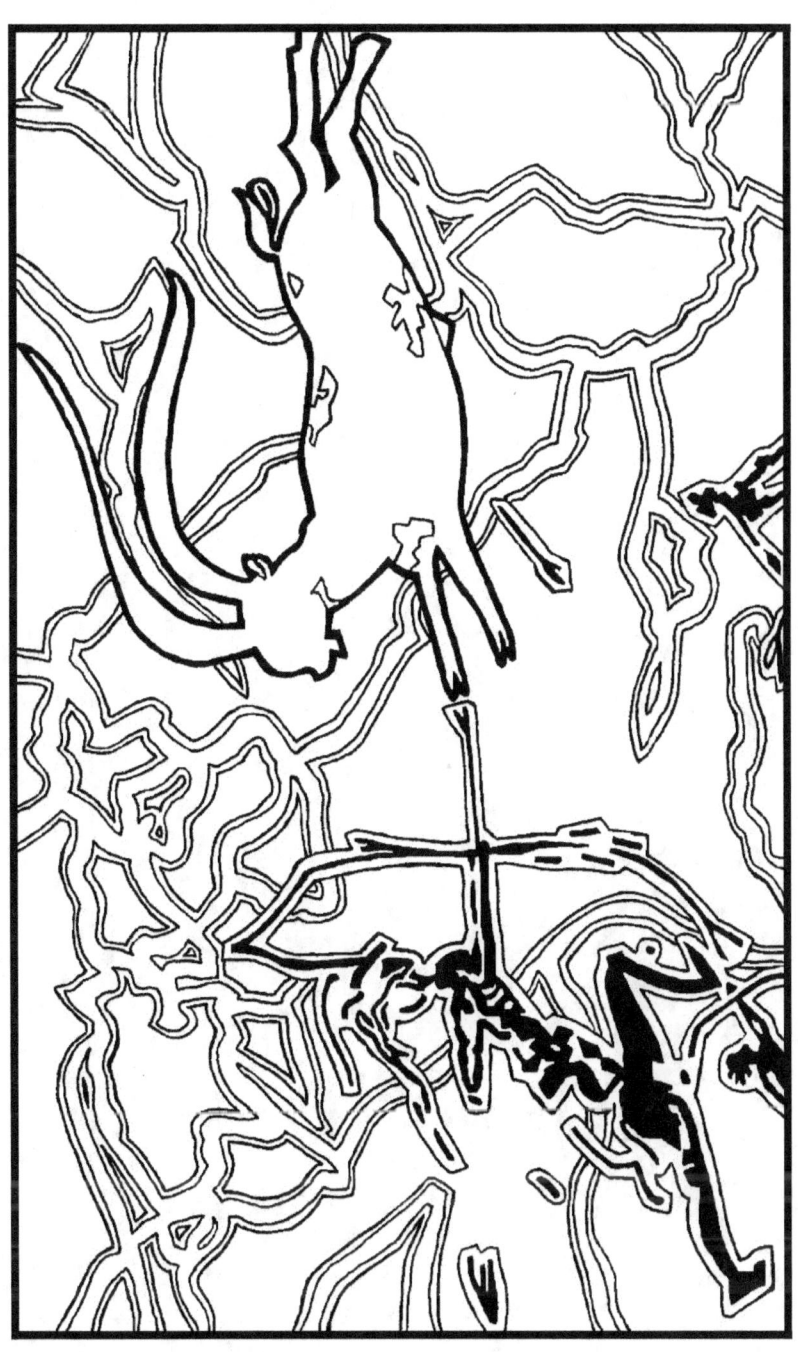